Canada

An Expat's Guide

Canada Immigration, Housing and Living Options, Work & Business, Family & Education, Retirement, Relocation Tips, Taxes & Banking, Essential Expat Guide and Much More!

By Tess Downey

Foreword

Aboriginal tribes were the ones who originally inhabited the land of Canada up until the time when Europeans started settling here around the 17th and 18th century. Canada today is still part of the British Commonwealth and a popular expat destination especially for Americans, and Europeans particularly the British and French nationals. Despite of its European heritage, Canada share many social and economic similarities with its neighboring country - the United States.

In fact, this is one of the reasons why US citizens are moving to Canada because aside from the close proximity to their home towns, the Americans share many traits with the Canadians.

If you are one of those American or European expats looking for a different kind of experience but don't want to adjust too much in terms of settling in, then Canada could be the perfect destination for you. Of course, there are many foreign nationals from all over the world who have now made the Maple Country their new home including Asians, Latin Americans, and even those living in Oceania.

Canada's economy is steadily growing over the past decade, and a strong economy means that the country is now ready to accept immigrants not just from the US or UK but also from all over the world. In fact, Canada is one of the top western countries that are ready to accept foreign nationals compared to other western countries, this is because of the legal requirements to become a permanent resident and social acceptance is relatively straightforward here.

Expats moving to the progressive and well – developed Maple Country will surely experience a diverse kind of lifestyle!

This book will provide you with plenty of information about how to settle in Canada as an expat, the amazing opportunities you can take advantage of, and how you can truly become one of them Canadians. After reading this book, you'll surely be able to do a smooth transition to the Maple Country!

Table of Contents

Welcome to the Maple Country!

Canada is best known for three things: hockey, mountains, and its maple syrup – although this is not entirely the reason why it's famously known as the 'maple country,' it sort of has something to do with the maple leaves and maple trees that abound in this place. Aside from those three things, Canada has gained reputation and popularity among expatriates because of their notable social programs, endearing economy, and of course, the warm welcome of its Canadian citizens despite of its 'cold ambiance.'

Canada is the second biggest country on earth! Its scope is very large especially in terms of land area. The Maple Country occupies the northern part of the globe (almost close to the North Pole), and it also has many amazing attractions that will surely make many tourists and foreign nationals want to settle here.

Canada is a country built by foreigners since the early times, and the good thing about it is that until today, it continues to serve foreigners from different parts of the world. In fact, it has one of the highest per capita rates in terms of immigration. The only hindrance for most expats is the visa application process (something that we will discuss in the next few chapters). However, since Canada has a small population, wherein majority of which are already retiring, it will definitely need to fill different kinds of jobs in a variety of industries to ensure that the economy keeps moving forward and upward.

This is a great advantage especially for those who are looking to move here because it means you'll have plenty of work opportunities.

Aside from its strong economy and growing job opportunities, the country is also abundant in terms of its natural resources. The financial and communication industries as well as the real estate industry are thriving in Canada. They have plenty of natural gas reserves and also a major producer of on – shore oil sands.

Perhaps one of the most important things to consider before moving here or anywhere in the world is how they'll be able to have steady salaries so that they can maintain their cost of living especially those with families. Compared to many rich western and eastern countries, the cost of living in Canada is quite reasonable – the only downside however, is the tax rates as it is very high. So even if you have a high salary, it will surely be reduced once tax rates are applied. But for most expats, they don't mind the high taxes, why?

Well, it's because citizens here can fully take advantage of it through the 'world – class' assets, facilities, and systems that are in place. The health insurance or healthcare system is excellent, the public school education is top – notched and citizens are generally well – taken care of.

Aside from all of this, Canada is perhaps one of the safest countries in the world! They have the lowest rates of petty crimes, national injustices, and were never the target of terrorist attacks and ill will. People here are also well – disciplined and well – known for being respectful and courteous.

The only downside for expats and also tourists are its cold climate. Those who are settling in the coastal areas and southern parts of the country will not suffer as much compared those who are heading in the north like the cities of Edmonton and Calgary as well as the provinces in the Prairie area because it'll definitely be freezing. This may be one of the major drawbacks especially for those expats who are not used to cold weathers; the temperatures usually drop below the normal freezing level during bad weathers and snow usually lasts for 6 months straight covering the entire ground and houses. It will literally feel like you're living in Antarctica most of the time, which is a problem for some expats because they will have trouble adjusting to this extreme climate.

Don't worry though because Canada has always been this way and people here have gotten used to the idea of extreme winter which is why most of its buildings are well – equipped. Corporate offices, apartments, malls, and residential areas can withstand the cold climate all year round! You'll be warm enough to enjoy the 'White Christmas' vibe that Canada brings.

Despite of its cold temperatures, many expats in Canada says that their quality of life have improved because most cities here offers a societal blend, social acceptance, and the spectacularly vibrant scenery. In fact, in 2017, three major cities in Canada including Toronto, Vancouver, and Ottawa are included in the top 20 Mercer Quality of Living.

Thanks to its European origins, and American influences, Canada is now better than ever. It has become a place where immigrants around the world can truly settle in because of its great economy, fantastic government system, world – class services, spectacular sceneries, accepting and warm society, and a peaceful place filled with maple syrup, cold mountains, and great hockey players!

Chapter One: An Overview of Canada

Moving to a new place is definitely a life – changing experience for anyone, usually though people moving to another country is not just after the new living experience or because they wanted to take advantage of the many benefits a country can offer, for some people they do it because they wanted to reinvent themselves in some way, get a fresh start or move on from whatever they left behind. Whatever your reasons may be, Canada is truly one of those countries that will force you to hit restart, thanks to its beautiful sceneries that boasts the many wonders of nature, the refreshing icy vibe, and that feeling of 'isolation' in many of its far – off region. It will make anyone reflect on where they are now in life and where they want to possibly go.

Aside from it being a great place for a fresh start, Canada also boasts many modern cities along with its natural reserves. You'll be given an opportunity to enjoy the outdoors while enjoying many modern conveniences. Canada is frequently lauded as the number one nation in the world including the United Nations especially in terms of the quality of living. It's no surprise for Canadians because their country had been one of the safest and most admired nations for many decades now. This is what primarily attracts expats and tourists all over the world. It's a prosperous nation – and that is just the tip of the iceberg!

In this chapter, you'll be given an overview about the Maple Country including its history, origin, and climate. You'll also learn briefly about its major cities, and provinces as well as its form of government, language, and the people's social norms and culture. Get ready to experience Canada in the flesh!

Canada in Focus

Canada is founded by three foreign nationals – the Aboriginals, the British, and the French. This goes to say that the country's immigration has played a key role in establishing the Canadian society that we now know today. Aboriginal natives are the ancestors who settled in the country way before European explorers discovered and arrived in Canada. The Aboriginal tribes are grouped into three; these are the Indian natives, the Inuits, and the Metis. These ancestors made very important contributions in Canadian society especially during the early days of its establishment.

On the other hand, "French Canadians" includes the so – called Quebecers, and Acadians which are found in small communities across the country that were formerly occupied by French colonists who settled in the area about 400 years ago. Don't be surprise if you find that Canadians in Quebec and those in the Atlantic region are speaking in French; their ancestors have brought with them the many great cultures and French traditions that most French Canadians still carry today. You'll soon find that Quebecers have quite a different culture and identity compared to other Canadians living in other areas.

Then there's the so – called "English Canadians" who are descendants of UK immigrants (British, Scottish, Irish, Welsh) who settled in Canada around the 17th to 20th century. Perhaps the main contribution of the British society in Canada is its way of governance. Canada's government has different systems in place inspired from the British parliamentary system and the constitutional monarchy.

The 200 years of multi – cultural blend of many of Canada's pioneers is the main reason why it has become one of the best countries in the world. Recently, new immigrants like the Asians are making its own contribution in helping build Canada's new and improved way of life. There are also many ethnic and religious groups living together and working harmoniously today. In fact, almost 20% of Canadians today were born in other countries. Canada values immigrants as part of its multi – cultural society. The diversity is what makes the Maple Country united for many centuries.

A Brief History of Canada

Canada is a country built by foreigners so to speak. The blend of native Indian tribes, British, French, and American culture is what made this country what it is today. Now, the Asians and other nationalities are making their own marks in improving the Maple Country. Let's look back at what went down in history so that you can appreciate its multi – cultural influences. Here's a brief timeline of Canada:

- 1497: John Cabot, an Italian navigator, discovered the shores of Cape Breton and Newfoundland in Canada.

- 1534: French explorer Jacques Cartier claimed the Gulf of Lawrence as one of France's territories.

- 1583: England proclaimed Newfoundland as one of its first colonies in Canada.

- 1600: Rival European countries including France, UK, and Denmark formed alliances to fight off the native Indians and conquer the place.

- 1627: New France was established as part of France's colonies in North America

- 1670: A London based company called Hudson Bay acquires the trading rights for areas whose rivers go into Hudson Bay.

- 1701: 38 Indian nations made a peace treaty with France that puts an end to the 20 years of diplomacy.

- 1756: The Seven Year War started between New France and British colonies in Canada. Quebec falls, and the English eventually conquered Montreal.

- 1763: Great Britain acquired all the colonies of France under the Treaty of Paris including New France that became under the colony of Quebec.

- 1774: Under the Quebec Act, the French language and the Roman Catholic religion were recognized.

- 1776 to 1780: Refugees from the American War settled in different places including Prince Edward Island, Ontario, Quebec, and Nova Scotia.

- 1791: Quebec was divided into two; the Lower Canada (present – day Quebec) and the Upper Canada (present – day Ontario).

- 1800: Europeans began moving to Canada including English, Scottish and Irish.

- 1812 - 1814: The War of 1812 began between the Americans and the British. The US failed to take Canada away from Great Britain.

- 1841: Establishment of the United Province of Canada including the East and West Canada.

- 1867: Establishment of Dominion of Canada; the states of Ontario, New Brunswick Nova Scotia, and Quebec.

- 1870: Manitoba was officially declared as the fifth province of Canada followed by Prince Edward Island, and British Columbia.

- 1885: The Canadian Pacific Railroad Transit is finally completed.

- 1898: Yukon River became one of the places for mining due to gold rush.

- 1905: Alberta and Saskatchewan were officially declared as one of the provinces of Canada.

- 1914: World War I broke out. Canada teams up with the British and French forces.

- 1931: Canada became autonomous as a country; the Statue of Westminster was built.

- 1939: World War II broke out. Canadian Army is active in Europe and the Atlantic.

- 1947: Canada is declared as equal status with Great Britain within the British Commonwealth.

- 1965: The present – day Canadian flag is adopted

- 1968: Pierre Trudeau wins the elections

- 1982: Great Britain granted Canada its independence; the country now adopted its new constitution and charter of rights.

- 1989: Establishment of free trade between Canada and U.S.

- 1993: Jean Chretien became the new Prime Minister, and was re – elected in 1997.

- 2006: Stephen Harper and the Conservative party won majority of the seats in the government, ending the 12 years of Liberal government in Canada.
- 2015 to Present: Justin Trudeau, eldest son of Canada's 15th Prime Minister Pierre Trudeau, became the newly – elected leader of the country.

Cities and Provinces in Canada

The capital of Canada is Ottawa. Ottawa is the 4th largest city, and it is located along the Ottawa River bordering Ontario and Quebec. Overall Canada has 10

provinces, and each has its own capital. The provinces or territories are also grouped into five regions. The top 3 largest and most popular cities in Canada are Toronto City located in Ontario, Vancouver City in British Columbia, and Montreal located in Quebec. These 3 cities comprise almost 1/3 of the Canadian population. Below are the list of the cities, territories, and provinces in Canada together with its capital and approximate population as of 2017.

Regions	Province	Capital	Population
Atlantic Provinces	Newfoundland (including Labrador)	St. John's	514,000
	Prince Edward Island	Charlottetown	140,000
	Nova Scotia	Halifax	921,000
	New Brunswick	Fredericton	751,000
Central Canada	Quebec	Quebec City	7,900,000

	Ontario	Toronto	12,850,000
Prairie Provinces	Alberta	Edmonton	3,645,000
	Manitoba	Winnipeg	1,200,000
	Saskatchewan	Regina	1,033,000
Northern Canada	Nunavut	Iqaluit	31,900
	Northwest Territories	Yellowknife	41,400
	Yukon Territory	Whitehorse	33,800
West Coast	British Columbia	Victoria	4,400,000

Geography and Climate

Being the second largest country in the world, Canada covers about 3.9 million square miles of land area bordering three of the largest oceans including the Pacific, Arctic, and the Atlantic. Overall Canada covers 200,000 km of coastline.

The Maple Country also shares two borders with the Northwest side of the world, and the United States. And because of its vast land area, it's not surprising that it contains different and beautiful landscapes and water areas. You can find lots of high mountains that locals love to trek in, various types of forests, grasslands, and frozen tundra that are home to many interesting animals like the grizzly bear. People also love doing many water – related activities here because the country is also filled with many lakes and rivers almost untouched by man – made developments.

In terms of climate, Canada has four distinct seasons including winter, summer, spring and fall. Below are the quick summary of when you can expect to experience these kinds of climate:

Spring Season

When: late February to late May

Temperatures: average temperature is above 0°C (32°F). Most cities in Canada still experiences snow storm during spring but you can see tulips start to bloom by this time.

Summer Season

When: June to August

Temperatures: Warm to very humid climate; daytime temperatures can hit from 20 degrees Celsius to 30 degrees (68 to 86 degrees Fahrenheit)

Common Areas:

- o **Central/ Eastern Canada** (including Toronto and Montreal): Hot and humid
- o **West Coast**: moderately warm (less humid throughout the day; has cool evernings)
- o **Northern Regions** (Whitehorse, Edmonton, Dawson City): cooler summers; quite sunny

Fall/ Autumn Season

When: September to November

Temperatures: slightly cooler temperatures that provides relief from summer's humidity. Days are shorter and leaves begin to turn into shades of red, yellow and orange in most cities. Best time to travel in Canada is during the autumn or fall season.

Winter Season

When: snow – covered ground almost like blizzard looking environment from December to February

Temperatures: Often hit below zero degrees - 32 to - 20°C except in the southwest area of British Columbia including

Vancouver and Victoria city as rain is more common here than snow.

Common Areas:

- o Rockies: experiences long winters
- o Calgary: does not get heavy snows compared to other cities
- o Banff, Canmore: expect around 2 feet of snow during the month of April.
- o Toronto and Montreal: experiences short but fierce winter season. Expect 8 inches of snow around January to February.

Some Tips for Newbie Expats:

- Most expats especially those coming from warm weather countries and even those with a winter season are very surprise with the Canadian winter. It is extremely cold even for an average local. Make sure to buy winter coats, gloves, hats, scarfs, and boots to keep you warm and protect you from the cold weather especially when going outside.

- Most houses and buildings in Canada have fireplaces, and as mentioned earlier the buildings are built to withstand such extreme weather. The only thing you have to worry about aside from scooping ice out of the driveway is how you can enjoy this literal winter wonderland!

Language

The native tongues of Canadians are English and French. There are about 18 million people, who speak in English as their first language, while 7 million speak French as their primary language. If you plan on settling in areas like Quebec, Nova Scotia, Newfoundland, and Prince Edward Island as well as in Ontario, Manitoba, and New Brunswick, then it's probably best that you learn a bit of the French language because the communities here are mostly made up of "French Canadians," it'll be very helpful especially if you want to connect with the locals.

Aboriginal languages and other variety of languages from Asian nationals are also spoken in Canada. Make sure to do a bit of research as to what groups of immigrants are mostly living in the area you're planning to settle in so that you'll have an idea about the language they're speaking, and maybe learn a tad about it. Don't worry though because the Federal Government of Canada requires services to be written or spoken in the country's official languages which are English and French.

Economy

Canada's strong and resilient economy is powered by three types of industries including those in the service industry, manufacturing industry, and natural resources.

The **Service Industry** comprises about 75% of Canadian jobs. It includes the following:

- Transportation
- Healthcare
- Banking
- Education
- Communications
- Construction
- Retail Services
- Tourism
- Government

The **Manufacturing Industry** is where products are being made and sold locally and around the world. This is the trading powerhouse of Canada. The United States is Canada's largest international trading partner. Products that are being manufactured in Canada include the following:

- Paper
- Aerospace Technology
- Machineries
- High Technology Equipment
- Clothing
- Food
- Automobiles
- Other Goods

Canada's **Natural Resource Industries** have played a key role in developing the economic and tourism branches of the country throughout history. A large percentage of Canada's exports like minerals, gas and oil come from natural resources, and many provinces also depend on these industries for their day to day life. Industries include the following:

- Forestry
- Fishing
- Energy
- Mining

Government

Canada's government system is a constitutional monarchy, a federal state and a parliamentary democracy. This section will give you a brief overview of the kind of government system that is in place so that you'll know how such laws and regulations play out in the Maple Country.

Levels of Government

There are 3 levels of government in Canada namely; Federal, Provincial, and Municipal.

Federal Government

Ottawa being the capital of Canada is where the Federal Government is based. It is mainly responsible for both the national and international affairs of the country. The Federal Government of Canada is headed by the Prime Minister, and is equal to that of a president in other countries. The federal government handles all matters concerning different departments including the following:

- National Defense
- Currency
- Banking
- Employment Insurances
- Foreign Affairs
- Shipping
- Postal Services
- Telephones

- Pipelines

- Aboriginal Lands and Rights

- Criminal Law

Provincial and Territorial Governments

The 10 provinces and 3 Canadian territories are each led by a Premier, and it also has its own elected officials that have the power to manage public lands, public laws, and carries out many intercommunity functions as identified by the Constitution Act of 1867 in the following fields or departments:

- Education

- Road Regulations

- Health Care

- Agriculture

- Immigration

- Natural Resources

Constitutional Monarchy

Canada is also a constitutional monarchy, thanks to British influences. The Queen or King of Canada is considered as the head of the state. Ever since 1600, when New France was founded, Canada has enjoyed Royal protection and patronage.

The King or Queen of Canada is also the Head of the Commonwealth (also called The Sovereign) which means that Canada is one of 16 countries under the sovereignty of His/Her Majesty of Great Britain – in this case, Queen Elizabeth II. Canada is one of the 53 countries that are part of the social, economic, and cultural advancements and interests.

Social and Cultural Norms and Etiquettes

Gender Roles

- Equality in gender roles in Canada is progressive but the process is quite slow and some form of bias still exists. As an example, men are still dominant when holding top positions in major industries like healthcare and the government.

- Men and women are both welcome to hold positions in the government, and they are equal in status.

- The gender roles of men and women are significantly changing with more men sharing household roles and child care.

Socialization

- Children in Canada are required to attend school until they reach the age of 16. Children can be home – schooled as long as it is in accordance with the government regulations.

- Parents are permitted to use physical means to teach discipline to their children but striking a child out of anger is not reasonable under Canada's law.

- If a child has done some sort of mischievous behavior, the parents will be responsible for it especially if the child is 12 years old and below. Usually, there'll be penalties depending on what the child did.

Meeting and Greeting

- It is usual for people to kiss both cheeks whenever they meet with a friend or has been introduced to somebody. This is more common in Quebec as this is something that the people adopted from the French culture.

- Some men may also kiss a lady's hand as a sign of respect and greeting.

- Generally, Canadians are polite, and respectful towards other people. They also expect other people to do the same.

- Canadians usually shake hands while maintaining eye contact with almost everyone once they arrive and depart at a meeting especially if it's a formal one.

- Men usually are the first one who initiates a hand shake when meeting women.

Gift Giving

- Generally, Canadians give out gifts during different occasions like the holidays and birthdays

- When invited to a house for dinner, one usually brings a box of chocolates, bottle of wine or flowers (except lilies because it is often used at funerals).

- When sending out flowers, Canadians especially those in Quebec send it to the one who invited them in advance or to the host's house.

- If you're going to buy a bottle of wine, make sure it is of the best quality, a rather expensive one especially if you're living in Quebec.

- Never hand out cash as a present

- Gifts are being opened once received.

Dining Manners

- Table manners are quite informal in Canada unless you're in a formal place or at a formal event

- It is quite formal if you're residing in Quebec

- When you're at a restaurant or a party, you should wait for the waiter or the host to lead you to your seat

- Don't begin eating until you are given a signal by the host or until the hosts begin.

- Don't put your elbows on the table while eating

- During formal events, the host is the one who gives the first toast, and the honored guest usually returns the toast at the end of the meal.

Taboos

- It's disrespectful if you point at people for no reason

- Don't confuse Canadians with Americans

- It is best to not initiate discussions regarding politics, religion, and other serious topics especially if you do not entirely know anything about it.

Business Culture and Etiquette

- The dress code in Canada when attending business meetings is the conventional suit and tie for men, and smart dress or suit for women.

- Address people as Monsieur or Madame especially if you're with high – class Canadians or those in the academe particularly in Quebec

- You can also use Mr. and Mrs. until you get to know the first name of the person you're talking to.

- During business meetings, it's important that you adhere to the time schedule. Meetings in Canada are well – organized, quite informal, and also relax even if serious matters are being discussed. Some could also be quite democratic wherein participants are given the freedom to contribute and engage in the discussion.

- When it comes to the style of management, Canadians are usually emphasizing egalitarianism. Managers and those with high positions should be treated with respect but employees or those in the lower rank are treated fairly and equally.

- Businesses are not really hierarchical; any employee's opinion regardless of their ranks in a company or establishment is valued and encouraged during decision making.

Chapter Two: Immigration

The federal and provincial government of Canada are always updating and further enhancing their immigration programs to better serve foreign nationals who wish to reside in the country, and also ensure that immigrants are well taken care of. Currently, there are around 60 immigration programs available to foreigners and would – be expats like yourself. This is not just targeted for individuals but also for their families. And for this reason, everyone's path to becoming a permanent resident in Canada will be unique because it will highly depend on the status of the potential immigrant and their families.

Other factors including their work, finances, businesses, investments, and various legal matters will definitely affect how you/ your family will acquire a permanent residency status.

The good news is that Canada is very open to foreigners and is widely accepting immigrants from all over the world. This chapter will provide you with an overview of the different programs that are available for different types of immigrants. You'll also be provided with a list of the general requirements for each kind of applicants. Keep in mind though that such requirements are subject to change, it's highly recommended that you always stay updated, and consult with professionals regarding the immigration matters.

Applying for immigration is one of the very first steps you need to do before even planning where you're going to stay or researching about other expat essentials is. The processing of papers and filing of documents that are needed for you to make a smooth transition will definitely take quite a period of time, energy, and money which is why this is a very crucial step. Once you're approved and ready to go, everything will be quite easier.

Some details may not be covered particularly for people who may have problems with their visas, passports or any other related citizenship issues, so it's up to you to consult with proper authorities in order to resolve that. You would want to make sure that everything is approved and documented properly so as not to have the possibility of being deported or have problems down the road once you've completely moved in.

Different Types of Immigration Programs in Canada

Skilled Worker Immigration Program

One of Canada's main goals in terms of immigration is to welcome newcomers particularly the skilled workers because they're the ones who will hugely contribute to the country's growing economy. Skilled workers who are permanent residents of the country are very valuable because they make up most of the workforce.

If you're planning to apply under the Skilled Worker Immigration program of Canada, you're goal is to not just find a permanent job in the country but also be able to acquire a permanent residency status wherein it will allow you to move to Canada with your immediate family.

As a professional or skilled employee, the route to permanent residency can vary depending on your situation, on your work contract, and the province where you and your family will reside.

There are three subcategories under the Skilled Worker Immigration program of Canada, learn about it to see which one is best suited for your situation as requirements and qualifications will be different for each. Below is the overview of the programs for foreigners who wish to join Canada's workforce and eventually obtain a permanent resident visa:

- **Federal Skilled Worker Program**: This is a program for those who have special work experiences, and those who wanted to have a permanent residency status in any of Canada's provinces or territories except Quebec.

- **Quebec Skilled Worker Program:** This is best suited for individuals who intend to find a job and reside in the province of Quebec. You need to submit applications and see if you're eligible under this program.

- **Provincial Nominee Program (PNPs):** This is a program that could fast – track your immigration papers because it allows an individual to acquire a provincial nomination certificate depending on where they will work or where they intend to live. Most provinces in Canada have their own set of requirements for such skilled workers which enable the potential immigrant to get their papers be processed quickly.

Family Class Sponsorship Program

The government of Canada has set up many ways for foreign nationals to not just find a job here but also reside in the country together with their families, thanks to the Family Class Sponsorship Program.

This is one of the most generous family programs that has been created by a first – world country which means to say that Canada is really committed in keeping families together as much as possible. Just like the Skilled Worker Immigration Program, the Family Class Sponsorship is also divided into different categories that will suit the needs of every family member. This includes the following:

- **Spouses and Common – Law Partners:** If you wanted to bring your spouse or partner to Canada, you will most likely be presented with a number of options on how both of you can acquire permanent residency, and it can be rather complicated. Therefore, each option should be weighed carefully. There are two categories under the Federal Spousal Sponsorship, these are Inland and Outland. Be sure to consult an immigration officer or lawyer so that they can explain to you the pros and cons of the different programs available. Of course, you need to ensure that your spouse or partner is eligible in order for their application to be accepted. You need to also meet the sponsorship requirements of Canada (ex: financial support) so that your application can be processed easily. You can also have the option of choosing programs under the Provincial Family Class Sponsorship for your spouse or common law partner.

- **Parents and Grandparents:** Through this program, you can now bring with your parents or grandparents. This is best suited for people who are still single or those who are unmarried. However, there's a yearly cap in the number of applications that'll be accepted. All you need to do is for you to meet the sponsorship requirements for your parents/ grandparents (since you'll be the one to sponsor them), and your parents/grandparents should also be able to meet the eligibility requirements needed which usually varies depending on the situation. Make sure to consult an immigration officer or lawyer to have you assess if this is the right program for you and your parents/grandparents.

- **Dependent Children:** If you are already a permanent resident or a Canadian citizen, and you wish to bring with you your dependent child/children (those below 18 years old), then you can do so under the Dependent Child Sponsorship program. Same rule goes, which means that your child should be eligible, and that you as the sponsor should also meet the sponsorship requirements.

- **Provincial Family Class Sponsorship Program:** Some province in Canada offers the Provincial Family Class Sponsorship to those relatives who were not able to meet the requirements of the federal programs. However, it's only being offered occasionally so the availability can vary, which means that you cannot choose to reside to other places. This type of sponsorship program is always subject to change so better consult an immigration officer or lawyer first so that you and/or your family can see the most suitable immigration program.

- **Super Visa Program:** This is for those immigrants who intended to bring their parents/grandparents to Canada. As mentioned earlier, there are certain limitations to the number of applications being accepted every year under the Parents/Grandparents Sponsorship program, so once the cap is reached, you can have the option to apply under the Super Visa Program. This however, only grants and extension of a multi – entry visa for up to 10 years for your parents/grandparents. This is more suitable for such relatives who do not wish to become a permanent residency but can come and reside in Canada for up to 10 years or until they have applied and got accepted under a different Family Class program.

Business Immigration

Canada also offers many programs that are aimed at attracting individuals who can contribute to the economy of the country. This usually includes entrepreneurs, self – employed, and investors who are looking to establish their businesses or companies in Canada or those who have a significant amount of money to invest in any of the local companies in the country. Such individuals can acquire permanent residency through the Business Class Immigration Programs.

Programs under the Business Class Immigration are targeted to further the economic sustainability of the country, and to also open more working opportunities to local and foreign workers. Below are some of the frequently asked questions about the Business Class Immigration Programs of Canada. If you have the entrepreneurial skill, the venture capital or the business acumen, then this is the best option for you and your family.

What programs under the Business Class Immigration should I consider if I'm ready to invest a significant amount in a Canadian business?

There are many possible programs for you to explore, the eligibility will highly depend on how much you'd be willing to invest in a Canadian company or establishment. Consider the following programs:

- **Quebec Immigrant Investor:** This is a program for individuals to wish to immigrate to Canada through making a passive investment that is government – secured.

- **Entrepreneur/ Provincial Nominee Program:** This is a program for those who are looking to a more active type of investment, which means that an individual will be required to not just invest in a Canadian business but also operate in it.

- **Entrepreneur Start – Up Visa Program:** This is mostly for those entrepreneurs who wish to establish a start – up company in Canada or for those who wanted to do their start – up operations in the country. The qualifications for this program is quite different than the other entrepreneurial/investor programs as this is more targeted for newbie companies that can potentially offer a sustainable company.

What if I wanted to operate or establish a business in Canada?

Usually, the eligibility requirements include your ownership experience (if you have previous businesses or are currently running a business in your home country) and your business management experience as well. You can be qualified under the different entrepreneurial categories aforementioned or under the Provincial Nominee Programs being offered at a federal level. Under the PNPs, it will usually require you to make an active investment (capital or business management skills) to businesses established or located in any of Canada's provinces that are currently offering such program. Consult an immigration officer or lawyer to see which program best suits you so that you can take full advantage of the many benefits. Requirement and eligibility are always subject to change so it's better to ask a professional or expert so that your application can be processed with ease.

What if I'm self – employed or well – established in my chosen field?

Canada welcomes self – employed people in different fields. You'll be given various options when it comes to immigration depending on your situation. Of course, one of the major requirements is your track record, and reputation in your chosen field. Consult an immigration officer or lawyer to see the best route to immigration you should take.

Quebec Experience Class (PEQ)

This program is for those immigrants or temporary residents who have previously studied or work in Quebec. Under this immigration program your application can be easily processed provided that you pass the needed requirements and you are eligible. The Quebec Experience Class is suited for foreign nationals who are students or have previously studied in Canada, and for those who have working experience in the province of Quebec.

Immigration to Quebec is usually a 2 – step process; applicants will need to apply for the Quebec Selection Certificate or the CSQ which allows an individual to immigrate in Quebec. After obtaining such document, the applicant must then submit an application to the Immigration, Refugees and Citizenship Canada (IRCC) for federal approval.

Once the applicant has successfully done that, and has been approved, he/she will then be issued the Permanent Resident Visa given by the Canadian Immigration. The Federal Immigration of Canada will be in charge of doing background checks as well as medical checks to the applicant and/or families/relatives of the applicant.

If for some reason you are not eligible under the PEQ program but have had studied or worked in Quebec, you could still try to apply through the Quebec Skilled Worker Program wherein a different set of requirements and eligibility may be in place.

Below are some general requirements for Foreign Students and Temporary Foreign Workers who are eligible under the Quebec Experience Class (PEQ)

For Foreign Students:

- The foreign students should have a degree or diploma issued by an educational institution that is recognized by the Quebec Ministry of Education within the past 3 years

- The student should have studied in an educational institution in Quebec for at least 2 years or have completed 1,800 hours of school work.

- The students should have completed a French course (advanced intermediate level) at a school in Quebec or if not, he/she should prove French ability through passing the standardized language test that is recognized and approved by Quebec's government.

For Temporary Foreign Workers:

- The worker should have 12 months of working experience (skilled, professional, and managerial) within the province of Quebec 24 months before the submission of their application.

- The foreign worker should be employed at the time of their application, and must also show legal status.

- The students should have completed a French course (advanced intermediate level) at a school in Quebec or if not, he/she should prove French ability through passing the standardized language test that is recognized and approved by Quebec's government. An alternative for this is if the foreign worker has completed the French language requirements as needed by their profession or occupation in Quebec.

Provincial Nominee Program (PNP)

Another fast – track option for foreign nationals to become a permanent resident is through the Provincial Nomination Program (PNPs). As mentioned earlier, this can be an alternative way for those who won't be able to meet the requirements for different categories under the federal programs. Primarily though, this is a program that allows Canadian provinces and territories to nominate foreign nationals (through a unique selection system) who wanted to move to Canada especially those who are looking to settle in a particular province or territory.

The provinces and territories' PNPs are anchored under the IRCC which allows these provinces to select foreigners that will meet the requirements that each has set for their own area. Such programs are created to welcome expats who wish to become permanent residents in a particular region or province which is why each PNP is uniquely tailored to the specific needs of the territory or state so that the local government can select applicants which could truly make a contribution within the community.

International Adoption

Permanent residents are also permitted to adopt children from other countries. The process is quite daunting since the government would want to protect the children's rights. It will usually involve conducting background checks of the family where the child/children will be adopted as well as the environment where the child/children were raised. There would be various legal issues involve including the Immigration office of Canada, the legal offices and departments concerning child adoption in other countries where the child was obtained, as well as the Hague Convention which is generally responsible for international adoptions. Canadians or permanent residents who intend to adopt children should also prove that they have the financial capability and commitment to raise a child and pursue their best interest.

General Requirement for Permanent Resident Visa

Once you have selected the right program for you, the next thing to do is to contact your nearest Canadian Embassy. The general requirements for permanent residency applicants include the following; do take note that these are subject to change without prior notice so make sure that you're updated:

- Medical Certificates (can vary depending on the visa program you selected)

- Criminal Record clearances from your local government in your home country

- Duly signed permanent residency visa application

- Application Fees

- Schedule of interviews with Canadian consulates

- Financial statements/ bank statements

- Working Contracts or Proof of Admission (if student)

- Other necessary documents

- Depending on your visa category, the following requirements may or may not be required, check with your nearest Canadian consulate or proper authorities:

- Original and photocopies of diplomas, identification cards/documents, other educational degrees obtained, birth certificates, marriage certificates, sponsorship letters, and other relevant documents that will be required for you to meet the criteria of the visa program you wish to apply in.

- Sufficient funds as proof that you can support yourself or that of your chosen sponsor (ex: parents, spouse, dependent child) during your stay in the country

- Skills assessment test

- Language test proficiency results

- Proof of refugee status

- Additional application/interview fees

Fees for Permanent Residency

Below is the breakdown of the fees that you may need to pay during your permanent residency visa application (updated as of 2017):

For Family Class Visa Program Applicants:

- Sponsorship Application (for the parents/child/relatives): **$75/application**

- Principal Applicant (for the one who will sponsor/the main immigrant): **$475**

- If the principal applicant is 18 years old and below, and is not considered under the category of a spouse/ common – law partner: $75 **(includes the dependent**

child, adopted child or the orphaned brother, sister, nephew, niece, grandchild).

- If the relative of the principal applicant is 19 years old and above or less than 19 years, and is considered a spouse/ common – law partner: **$550**

- If the relative of the principal applicant is less than 19 years, and is not considered a spouse/ common – law partner: **$150**

Important Note: Fees for the principal applicants and their relatives under the category of Family Class Sponsorship program is payable together with the sponsorship fee once the sponsor/principal applicant submits the sponsorship application.

For Entrepreneurs, Self – Employed, and Investor Class Visa Programs Applicants:

- Principal Applicant: $1,050

- If the relative of the principal applicant is 19 years old and above or less than 19 years, and is considered a spouse/ common – law partner: **$550**

- If the relative of the principal applicant is less than 19 years, and is not considered a spouse/ common – law partner: **$150**

For Other Class Visa Program Applicants:

- Principal Applicant: **$550**

- If the relative of the principal applicant is 19 years old and above or less than 19 years, and is considered a spouse/ common – law partner: **$550**

- If the relative of the principal applicant is less than 19 years, and is not considered a spouse/ common – law partner: **$150**

Chapter Three: Best Expat Districts in Canada

Canada boasts many amazing cities and provinces for foreign nationals looking to move to the country because of abundant working opportunities and high quality of living. Since you're already preparing to become an immigrant in Canada, I'm pretty sure that you already have an idea of where you would want to settle in with your family or relatives. It's also possible that you have top choices, but are still considering many factors.

This chapter will help you decide the important things you need to consider before deciding to move to a certain area. You'll also be provided with a list of the top 10 best cities and provinces in Canada.

Do keep in mind though that it's also best if you can inquire or asks family members/friends who are already living in Canada (if any) or check out different expat forums online so that you can have an idea if a certain area your eyeing best suit your needs and that of your family. Canada is a diverse and very large country in terms of land area; you can find many municipalities and cities within each province which means that you have many options to choose from. It's always ideal to visit the country first or do a tour of the different states in Canada so that you can truly determine if the place is right for you.

In this chapter, you will be given an overview of each of the top cities in Canada where expatriates commonly live. You'll also know the pros and cons for each as well as the general cost of living. Before deciding where to rent or buy a house, make sure to explore and do your own research so that you can ensure that you'll get the best possible Canadian living experience.

Factors You Need to Consider When Choosing a City/Province

There are many factors to consider when choosing the best place for relocation. Make sure to weigh the pros and cons of each factor against your ideal city/province. Check out the following important things to consider as a potential Canadian immigrant:

- The Immigration Visa Program or Class Categories
- Rate of employment
- Proximity of your work place to your ideal home
- Population (including the percentage of expats living in your ideal city or area)
- Cost of Housing
- Cost of Living
- Accessibility/ Transportation
- Weather

- Crime rates (if any)
- Average Household Income
- Overall Amenities (malls, grocery stores, hospitals, police stations, gas stations, banks, food places, highways, religious places, landmarks etc.)
- Education/ nearby schools
- Place of work/business

Important Note: If you are considering becoming a permanent resident, many expats usually settle in British Columbia, Alberta, and also Ontario.

Where do Most Expats Live and Why?

Most western and Asian expatriates looking to migrate to Canada usually settle in the following provinces:

- Quebec
- Ontario
- Alberta
- British Columbia

Many foreigners find themselves settling in these places simply because it's in close proximity to natural resources such as mountains, lakes, parks which is away from the hustle and bustle of the city or because the quality of living here is at its best which means the employment rate is great, it's close to many amenities, very accessible, and not just expat – friendly but also family – friendly locations.

There are some expats who deliberately choose to not settle in places that's close to cities because they wanted to either explore the spectacular and breathtaking sceneries that this great place has to offer or to just simply enjoy living every day without experiencing the 'busyness' of city – life. Despite of not being near the city, expats still get the same access to various services such as medical needs, housing needs, educational needs, and other basic necessities.

Of course, the cost of living in remote places is also much cheaper compared to residing in the city, which is already an advantage in itself because you can get to maximize your finances. Usually, foreigners who are retirees, and those youngsters who are looking for an adventure are the ones settling in far – flung places.

Top Canadian Cities Where Expats Live

Here's the list of the top 10 Canadian cities and provinces that is best suited for soon to be Canadian immigrants like yourself. We'll give you a bit of an overview about the city as well as its pros and cons.

Quebec

Quebec is famously known in Canada as *La Belle Province* (beautiful province), and has earned its reputation of being the "Europe of North America." It is the largest province or state in the country with a total population of around 8 million people and counting. Quebec is well – known for its vast forests, mountains, and waterways. This is the only province in Canada that carried on the French tradition and culture. French is also the official language of the province.

As mentioned earlier, if the province of Quebec is the place you wanted to settle in, make sure that you apply under the appropriate visa programs suited for immigrants looking to stay in Quebec as there would be different requirements, eligibility, and process for your immigration applications. The top 2 cities in Quebec for expats are the following:

- Gatineau, Quebec
- Brossard, Quebec

Gatineau, Quebec

The city of Gatineau can be found in the northern part of the Ottawa River, making it part of the National Capital Region (NCR). It's also the 4th biggest city in Quebec with a population of around 265,000. There are around 40,000 expats who arrive and settle in the Gatineau area, they are mostly Asians (Chinese, expats from South Asian countries), Africans, and foreigners from the Middle East making it one of the most diverse cosmopolitan cities in the country.

Popular Expat Neighborhoods:

- Lakeview Terasse
- Centre Town
- Lower Town
- Byward Market

Pros:

- Cheaper cost of living
- Cheaper daycare costs (if you have children)
- Lower tax breaks for parents
- Lower income taxes
- Cheaper Housing (usually comes with bigger lots)
- Expats will learn about the French culture and can be quite fluent in speaking French which could also be an advantage when finding jobs in Quebec.

- Many people live in Gatineau but work in Ottawa as it is in close proximity with each other.

Cons:

- Due to lower income tax, you'll have fewer options when it comes to healthcare needs and doctors
- The language can also cause a bit of stress in your day to day living, if you don't learn to speak in French or if you're not fluent also in English.

Brossard, Quebec

Brossard is the commercial hub near Montreal, and is lauded as one of the most highly diverse cities in Quebec and in the country. It's located in the Monteregie Region of Quebec and also part of Montreal. Even if French is the official language (since it's still part of Quebec) there are many minority languages present in Brossard such as English, Spanish, Persian, Chinese, Cantonese and Arabic.

The residential areas in Brossard have many apartment buildings and also single – detached homes.

It is near 4 municipalities connected through biking paths including the following:

- Saint – Lambert
- Carignan
- La Prairie
- Longueil

Pros:

- High – paying jobs; low unemployment rates
- Affordable housing
- Cultural diversity
- 36% of immigrants live here
- Generous income taxes
- Has access to different municipalities
- Expats will learn about the French culture and can be quite fluent in speaking French which could also be an advantage when finding jobs in Quebec.

Cons:

- Due to lower income tax, you'll have fewer options when it comes to healthcare needs and doctors

- The language can also cause a bit of stress in your day to day living, if you don't learn to speak in French or if you're not fluent also in English.

Ontario

Immigrants and even Canadians choose to settle in Ontario due to many reasons, one of which is because this is where the capital of Canada is located, and it's one of the highly – renowned places not just in the country but also in the world. It's a province that is environmentally – friendly even if it's a city – center. This is also the place where many services and amenities abound compared to other Canadian provinces. Ontario also has lots of services and family programs targeted for new expats or immigrants to help them settle in their new life and have the best Canadian living experience.

Another factor why immigrants love to settle in Ontario is because of the weather because compared to other places, people living in Ontario is getting more than enough sun so to speak but sometimes it's also a disadvantage. Aside from this, many working opportunities are being offered in Ontario, the official language is English, and it's mostly a place of diversity. This is where you can find one of the largest populations of immigrants from all over the world.

The top 4 cities in Ontario for expats are the following:

- Ottawa
- Waterloo
- Burlington
- Guelph

Ottawa

Ottawa is the capital of Canada. It's located in the eastern part of Ontario bordering Gatineau, Quebec, and sitting on the side of the Ottawa River and Rideau River. The climate in Ottawa is quite sunny but it also has long winters, and the city experiences drastic temperature changes especially during spring and fall seasons. The largest population of expats here are Chinese.

Ottawa bagged much recognition from different national and international bodies; Mercer ranked Ottawa City as the 14th Best City in the World, and the 2nd Best City in the Americas. Ottawa holds one of the longest records for being the #1 Best City in Canada according to MoneySense Magazine, and many international websites. The city is the 2nd cleanest in Canada and 3rd internationally by Mercer, and 4th cleanest city out of 300 cities worldwide according to Forbes. And because this is where the capital is located, there are many job opportunities for immigrants and locals here making it as one of the highest household income cities in Canada.

Pros:

- Family – oriented city
- Has a laid – back kind of lifestyle
- Quiet and peaceful
- Low crime rates
- Great healthcare services
- Employment rate is very high
- Plenty of different job opportunities
- Has high average household incomes ($89,000/year)
- Has many emerging start – up companies (earning its nickname as the "Silicon Valley of the North"
- Top – notched education systems and universities
- Public transport system is great
- A bike – friendly city

- Has plenty of opportunities for outdoor activities
- Ideal for expats with families

Cons:

- The housing is quite pricey compared to Montreal and Edmonton but still lower compared to Toronto and Calgary
- The summers are too hot (extreme heat); the winters are very cold and long
- The city has no subway/light rail
- Lack of exciting nightlife

Waterloo

Waterloo City is one of the smallest 3 cities in the Regional Municipality. It is located in the southern region of Ontario. There are about 25% expats living in Waterloo, Ontario. The main reasons why immigrants settle here instead in the capital is because the way of life is much exciting, diverse, and also thriving. Plus, people can choose if they want to stay in a mid – sized city or in the countryside. This is perfect for those who wanted to be in close proximity to the city – center but also have the luxury of a countryside kind of lifestyle.

Pros:

- Many employment opportunities particularly in manufacturing and technology
- Has world – class universities, modern colleges, and top – notched educational institutions
- Has a mix of both rural and urban living and lifestyle
- You can have plenty of outdoor and recreational activities like hiking and skiing
- A city filled with immigrants from all over the world thereby making you learn different cultural experiences
- Waterloo is home to many world – class talents that produces innovative products and research
- Has cheaper cost of living and housing compared to Ottawa.

Cons:

- The summers are too hot (extreme heat); the winters are very cold and long
- Can be quite far from the many amenities like high – end malls or food places.

Burlington

Located on the side of Lake Ontario is Burlington. It is part of the Halton Region alongside with communities like Milton, Oakville and Halton Hills. It's just about 30 – 45 minute drive to Toronto, Canada's biggest city. The Halton Region is one of the safest places in Canada and in the Toronto area. There are about 30% expats living in this area because of its central location, amazing natural scenery, and safe neighborhoods.

Pros:

- One of the best places for hiking in the world! Hikers can hike in the Bruce Trail and the Niagara Escarpment
- Quite a rural place but still has a high quality of life
- Has huge park lands covering a total of 580 acres
- Affordable housing (average price for single – detached homes is just around $555,000
- Has many job opportunities particularly in the manufacturing and automotive

Cons:

- The local area does not have many amenities (such as high – end malls/stores or many dining options)
- Has cold and dry winters, and very humid summers

Guelph

Guelph is in the southwestern region of Ontario with a population of just around 120,000. It is also known as the Royal City. It's in close proximity with downtown Toronto and in Waterloo.

Perhaps the main reason of why you should relocate here is because this is the place where you can find jobs easily. Since it's only a small city and the population is still quite small (but growing robustly), job competitions are fairly easy compared to other cities like Toronto and Ottawa. It has very low unemployment rate, and have a strong, long – term and abundant working opportunities waiting for immigrants and locals alike. It's also the 5th fastest growing city in Canada which means the local economy is steadily growing.

Pros:

- Very low crime rates

- Very clean environment

- The quality of living is high

- One of the highest employment rates in Canada despite of its small size and population.

- Has a diverse population; mostly dominated by British. Other minorities include Filipinos, Americans, Arabs, Chinese, Japanese and Latin Americans.

- Has many job opportunities especially in manufacturing and education sectors.

- Has many amazing and important landmarks like the Hanlon Creek Park, Wellington Street Nature Sites, Exhibition Park and the Royal City Park.

- Located between 2 rivers namely; Speed River and Eramosa River which provides plenty of water – related outdoor activities for family and friends

Cons:

- The local area does not have many amenities (such as high – end malls/stores or many dining options)
- Has cold and dry winters, and very humid summers so it will definitely take some time for one to get accustomed to the weather especially if you're an expat coming from warmer countries.

British Columbia

There are two cities/areas in British Columbia where most expats relocate into, these are; the city of Delta, and Saanich District. British Columbia is part of Vancouver, where the main downside is the cost of living, because Vancouver is one of the most expensive provinces in Canada.

In terms of expat populations, British Columbia is where most Chinese and Asian natives reside, and this is mainly because of the warmer weather. Compared to other cities in Canada, immigrants love British Columbia because of its mild col weathers. Winter in this province is not extremely cold compared to other places like Ontario and several provinces in the northern region, needless to say, the cold climate is quite bearable, and the places within British Columbia are not heavily filled up with snow during the winter season.

The top 2 cities in British Columbia for expats include the following:

- City of Delta
- Saanich District

Delta

Delta is under the municipality of British Columbia, and its location is also part of the greater Vancouver area. Delta city is at the southern part of Richmond and Washington, and it's also along the shores of Fraser River.

There are about 23% expats residing in this area, most of which are from Asian countries. Delta abounds in agricultural areas, which is why there are lots of working opportunities here related to farming, and it's also the biggest municipality in Vancouver.

This is a great place for expats who have been used to living in somewhat rural areas in their home country, and also a great place for those who loves hiking, cycling, picnics, island hopping, the wildlife, and other outdoor activities. The largest container terminal in the country can also be found here.

Pros:

- Offers a rural kind of lifestyle
- Has lots of open spaces and wide land areas perfect for outdoor activities

- Average household income is about 30% higher than the average income in other cities
- Abundant in farmlands and wetlands thereby enabling residents to always have access to fresh produce
- Aside from farming, opportunities also abound in other sectors including energy, communication, transportation, tourism, and manufacturing.

Cons:

- Has quite a small population (about 100,000)
- Cost of living is higher since it is located in Vancouver
- Cost of housing is very expensive, though compared to other Vancouver places, the Delta City has significantly lower housing rates, though still pricey compared to other Canadian provinces. (approx. $436,000 - $1,000,000)

Saanich District

Another go – to place of newcomers in British Columbia is the Saanich District. A large part of it is located also in the greater Victoria region. The population is also quite small (around 110,000) compared to other cities but since the land area is relatively smaller, it is one of the most populated area in the Capital Regional District.

This is a place where you can find a variety of professionals such as entrepreneurs, skilled workers, and artists. Usually, expats living here are quite rich because it's either they have a business in Canada or because they have high – paying jobs as the cost of living here is extremely high.

This is where you can find the renowned University of Victoria as well as other famous parks like the Mount Douglas Park, Mount Tolmie Park, and Gyro Park to name a few. It's also bordered by 6 municipalities with Victoria being the capital.

Pros:

- Has great transportation systems (Saanich district has more than 700 bus stops, and also has many paths and trails for cyclists)
- Has a diverse and growing economy which makes the city a good place for foreign investors
- Has many highly skilled workers
- Quality of living is top – notch, some people even say that it's incomparable with other Canadian cities (but you should be willing to pay the price).
- Has plenty of parks, waterways, and mountains perfect for those looking for an adventure
- One of the most environmentally friendly cities in British Columbia

Cons:

- Cost of living is very high; wages are also lower here compared to Montreal and Toronto
- Housing costs and tax breaks are also very high
- Weather is quite favorable

Alberta

Alberta is the one of the best relocation destination for expats with children or for those immigrants who wanted to take their other family members with them. The quality of living here is also great because the cost of living and housing is quite affordable, there are lots of job opportunities for different sectors, the local economy is robust, the education system is top – notched, it's crime rate is very low, the province is environmentally – friendly, and Canadians and immigrants alike are very welcoming here.

This is where you can also find lots of international establishments ranging from food places to popular malls and branded boutiques. The immigrants living here is a combination of Europeans, Americans, and Asians making it one of the most diverse places to live in. You'll surely get to adapt and learn different culture. This is also where lots of festivities are being held. It's a great place to travel and to spend time with your family. It's an urban lifestyle with a touch of rural living.

The top 3 cities in Alberta for expats include the following:

- St. Albert
- Edmonton
- Calgary

St. Albert

St. Albert was ranked as the #1 Best Place to Raise Kids (MoneySense Canadian Magazine). It's the most family – friendly city, the safest, and also one of the most prosperous areas in Alberta province and in the whole country. It has a population of about 65,000 residents both locals and immigrants. Another great factor why foreigners love settling here is because the city is flourishing, and many amenities are within reach. Other cities like Edmonton is just a few minutes away. It's also voted as one of the healthiest cities in Canada because people here love to exercise and eat healthy.

Pros:

- Low unemployment rate with high average household income in the country.
- Crime rates are relatively low
- Cost of living and housing expenses are affordable
- One of the cleanest city in the world
- Residents have great access to healthcare
- Weather is much favorable all year round
- Has many top – notch educational institutions
- Very welcoming locals
- Has about 2,500 and counting business establishments creating plenty of job opportunities.
- Has breathtaking sceneries and natural reserves perfect for various outdoor activities.

Con:

- Perhaps the only con is if this is not the place where you wanted to settle in for personal reasons.

Edmonton

Edmonton is the capital city of Alberta, and it's a favorite relocation area of immigrant workers because of its thriving economy that relies heavily in the gas and oil industries. Edmonton is located in the northern part of the Saskatchewan River, and also the 2nd biggest city in Alberta with a population of about 900,000.

This is where most European immigrants settle in including the British, Germans, French, Irish and Scottish. Other minorities make up about 22% of the population. It's also family – friendly, and has a very welcoming vibe. Edmonton is also known as the Festival City as many events are being held here all year round.

Pros:

- Expats take advantage of the excellent school system in Edmonton as this is where one of the oldest and largest universities in Canada are located – the University of Alberta. Foreign students looking to get a degree here allow them to avail government loans or apply for grants so that they can attend school.

- There are also many urban communities that abound in Edmonton, making it the 6th largest metropolitan area.

- Edmonton also has its own international airport, home to many large parklands, river valleys, and wide streets (where elm trees abound).

- Has many working opportunities within the city and also areas near the city

- There are lots of public and private golf courses which are perfect for those retired expats.

- Edmonton hosts many festivals, concerns, and multicultural events. Skiing and skating is also very popular during winter.

Cons:

- Has suffered economic recession over the past few years
- Housing options are quite limited

Calgary

Calgary has the highest percentage of expats than most cities in Alberta. The culture and communities here are very diverse due to different immigrants residing here. Many sporting events, concerts, and music festivals are also being held here from professional sports, pop culture to rock and roll music and the likes. It's also one of the most aesthetic cities in Canada because of its many historical buildings and magnificent architecture. Some of the things you should try visiting once you get here is the Husky Tower (one of the tallest building in Canada), the Calgary Stampede (a world – renowned landmark), Spruce Meadows (where show – jumping contests are being held), International Avenue, and there rotating restaurants which provides visitors with a spectacular view paired with delicious food.

Pros:

- It's a safe, environmentally – friendly, family – friendly, and one of the healthiest cities in Canada.

- Has many amenities like multicultural shops, international restaurants, international malls, world – class resorts, and other high – end establishments.
- Give residents an access to the breathtaking views of the Rocky Mountains since it is in close proximity to Banff and Canmore region.
- Has plenty of outdoor activities like skiing, snowboarding, trekking, ice – climbing etc.
- Housing is affordable with an average price of $458,000. Residents also have lots of options like single – detached styled homes, historic types, renters, and multi – family houses.

- There are lots of food trucks, food hubs, and international cuisines being offered since this place is filled with immigrants from different culture
- The weather is very favorable and sunny all year round.

Con:

- Has suffered economic recession over the past few years

Cost of Living in Canada

Most cities and provinces in Canada is quite affordable in terms of living and housing expenses. Perhaps the only two most expensive cities for average income earners are Toronto, Ontario and also anywhere in Vancouver/ British Columbia. Depending on the city, state or town you choose to settle in, it's essential that you know how much your day to day expenses will be before you decide to move.

Here's a breakdown of everything you might need when you relocate to Canada. The currency is in Canadian dollars, so just convert these items in your national currency so you can have a gauge at the costs of each. This section will not cover every single thing, this is just to give you an idea of how much items could cost. Do keep in mind that the cost of living may be higher if you're buying from branded stores, international depots or high – end malls.

Food	Average Cost (Canadian Dollars)
Lunch with drinks in Restaurants (business areas)	$17
Fast Food Combo Meal	$10
1 litter of milk	$2.50
12 eggs	$4.05
1 kilogram of tomatoes	$4
1 kilogram of potatoes	$2.40
1 bottle of red wine	$18
Bread (good for 1 day)	$2.35

Clothes	Average Cost (Mex Peso)
1 pair of jeans (branded)	$67
1 dress/ top dress (branded)	$55
1 pair of rubber shoes (branded)	$113
1 pair of leather shoes (branded)	$145

Transportation/ Commute	Average Cost (Mex Peso)
1 liter of gas	$1.18
Ticket for public transportation (taxis, buses, trains for 1 month)	$113

Personal Care/ Utilities	Average Cost (Mex Peso)
1 month worth of electricity, gas, heaters etc.	$107 more or less
1 month of Internet connection	$55 (can vary depending on your plan)

TV (Flat Screen - 40")	$487
Microwave	$160
Cleaning help (per hour)	$23
Antibiotics (1 box)	$22
Deodorant (50 ml)	$5.08
Shampoo (400 ml)	$5.38
Toothpaste	$2.77
Toilet Paper (4 rolls)	$3.05
Medical Checkup (private doctor)	$81
Gym membership (1 month; business district)	$60
Movie tickets (for 2)	$27
1 beer (local pub)	$52
Dinner for two in a fine dining (complete meal)	$90

Top 10 Most Expensive Cities/Provinces in Canada

Here is a quick of list of the top 10 most expensive cities in Canada:

#1: Vancouver

#2: Toronto

#3: Mississauga

#4: Calgary

#5: Ottawa

#6: Edmonton

#7: Victoria

#8: St. John

#9: Saskatoon

#10: Regina

Chapter Four: Housing and Estate Planning

Whether you are a retiree, you have a family, or

you're someone looking for a one – of – a– kind of

adventure, you'll need to ensure that you will be well –

accommodated in the province you chose so that you can

easily adjust to your newfound home! Learning the pros and

cons of your possible living destination, weighing in the

estimated costs of living, and considering the number of

immigrants in your chosen area is all essential before you decide about what kind of house you're going to acquire or how you're going to acquire it. It's very important that you and your family consider all the options in terms of housing and properties.

This chapter will give you an overview of how an expat like you, whether you're planning to become a temporary or permanent resident, can acquire a house and/or properties in Canada.

Renting vs. Buying

Keep in mind that you're not just going to buy or rent a place, you're investing your hard – earned money. This is also where you'll be spending most of your time, so better be wise, and really weigh everything or consult the right people before investing or committing to this huge undertaking.

A great way for you to weigh your options before doing any investments is to see all the possible pros and cons such as the type of house, the method on how to acquire it, the location, the overall value of the property, and other important things concerning real estate. It's best to set your own standards when making these decisions as it will definitely vary based on you/your family's needs.

Whether you're renting or buying a place, ensure that it will match your ideal housing/ accommodation plans. You can include different factors such as the following:

- Financial capacity and investment value (insurances, payment terms, appreciation, estate planning etc.)
- Meet your purpose (temporary/permanent resident/ with family/for work convenience etc.)
- Meet your standards (aesthetics/location)
- Enable you to have easy access to your basic necessities (transportation/amenities)
- Make you and your family truly 'feel at home'

The last thing you want is to settle in an area you like but not stay in a house you feel comfortable living in. Sometimes expats, because of their excitement to buy a new house in a new country, find themselves unhappy after the fuzz is over because they made poor decisions and lacked proper planning.

Housing Options in Canada

Rental Apartments

- Apartments that are usually in a single housing unit or in a building.
- Apartments in Canada can accommodate a family of 3 to 4 (depending on the size of the apartment for rent).
- It has one to three bedrooms on average

- If you rent a 'bachelor unit,' it only has a single bedroom and can accommodate 1 to 2 persons; comes with living rooms, small dining/kitchen area, terrace/balcony (depends if you're on a building or if the housing unit has one)
- Typically cheaper than renting in condominiums located in high – rise buildings
- Has more privacy compared to rental rooms.

Rental Rooms

- Sometimes owners of large houses divide their homes into many private bedrooms and rent it out
- The main downside perhaps is that usually people share a kitchen or even a bathroom.
- Lacks in privacy compared if you rent your own apartment
- Not ideal for immigrants with families
- Much cheaper compared when renting apartments or condos since you'll pretty much be paying for a bedroom/s only, and the cost is split among the other renters.

Condominiums

- Condos are located in building divided into many units

- Quite pricey compared to renting out apartments or rooms especially if the building is newly built

- Renters will not just pay for the monthly fees of the unit but also to the owner of the condominium itself because the building needs to be well – maintained and repaired.

- A fairly good choice for temporary/permanent residents or travellers who needs to stay for a longer period in Canada. This is also ideal for solo expats and even those with families or first – time homebuyers because it's still quite cheaper compared to buying a house and lot.

- Provides 24/7 security, usually comes with furniture, and also has added amenities like pools, gym, rooftop areas, lounge areas, parking spaces etc.

House and Lot

- Houses in Canada are usually single – detached house with relatively bigger lots. There are also semi – detached types, and townhouses (house that shares walls).

- You can also have the option of just buying a lot and build your own style but of course this is way more expensive in terms of building costs and labor.

- Purchasing a house is ideal for anyone who wanted to become a permanent resident in Canada as you can hold it for the long term, pass it down to your chosen heir/s, and even sell it as an investment.

- Real estate taxes, purchasing price, other annual fees, and mortgages will certainly vary depending on the province or city you chose. The top places where housing is very expensive includes Toronto, Ontario, and Vancouver.

Renting in Canada

If you're going to rent a house in Canada, you will be called the 'tenant' and the owner or manage of the property is your 'landlord.' Your landlord/ property manager/ superintendent are the one in charge in collecting the rental payments and also the management/maintenance of the building or house.

Renting is very ideal for expats especially if you're still building your savings or if you just started working. Acquiring a house and lot is going to always be way expensive than renting, and you'd have more headaches when it comes to maintenance so to speak. Perhaps the only downside when renting is that you'd never get to have your own property.

The responsibilities of the landlords and tenants will definitely vary in different cities or provinces. Make sure that you know the related laws in place for the area where you want to settle in as well as the rental process. It's also best that you consult with a real estate agent or ask relatives (if any) regarding the rental process.

Here are the general responsibilities of the tenants and landlords:

The landlord is responsible for the following:

- Collects the rental payments every month (or the payment terms you've agreed to).
- Keep the house or building well – maintained, secured, and in good condition
- Provides the furniture, appliances, facilities, and other amenities included in the rent
- Handling and paying for maintenance/repairs if your unit/house needs one.
- Provides the housing contracts, proper notices to the tenant

The tenant is responsible for the following:

- Paying the rent on the agreed due dates and in full
- Keeping the house/ unit/ area clean and well – maintained

- Calling the landlord if anything needs to be repaired or serviced

Important Note: If you think the landlord/tenant is not meeting his/her responsibilities or if any problems/issue arises, it's best that you reach out to the authorities in your municipality or province.

Guidelines when finding a place to rent

- Location and the cost of the unit/house for rent is the most important things you need to really consider. Ensure that the place you choose is quite close to your work, has easy access to transportation, schools, and other services you'll need.

- Once you've chosen a district or neighborhood, you can now start searching for units or houses that are available for rent. Just look for rental signs, check classified ads, ask people in your community, or inquire in shops/community centers. Of course, it'll be easier if you have relatives or friends because they can recommend you to certain rental places. You can also check online – go to expat forums, immigrant websites, or social media. Another option when finding one is to pay a rental agency so that they can help you find your ideal home, and save time and energy as they're the ones who'll handle the logistics.

- Make sure to have a few choices before deciding which one you should rent so that you can do pricing comparison and also let your family weigh in if this is the right place to stay.

- Once you've decided, it's time to check the place out. Make sure to prepare a list of questions for the landlord, and also thoroughly check if the house has complete amenities or in great condition so that you can also compare with other houses.

Questions to Ask Your Landlord:

- Are the utilities and appliances included in the rent? If not, how much will it cost per month?
- Does it come fully – furnished?
- Can I make home changes like painting the walls or decorating the house?
- (For those with pets or are smokers) Are pets, smoking, and is party activities allowed?
- Is there a designated area where I can smoke or is there a curfew?
- (For those with cars) Is there a parking, and is it included in the rent? If not, how much is the extra cost?
- Who are the other tenants and what are they like?
- Who owns/maintains the property?
- (For rental apartments) Is there storage locker or bicycle storage? How much is the extra cost? How secure is it?

Important Reminders:

- o Landlords in Canada usually ask you to give out references from your previous landlord or other contact information for references. This is to ensure that you will also be a good and responsible tenant.

- o Landlords will also ask your financial capacity, what your job is, where you work, and even check your credit history to gauge if you're a responsible payor.

- o If you're a newcomer and recently had a job, and obviously cannot provide a reference, it's best to ask for assistance from several immigrant organizations in your city or province.

Signing a Lease

Once you've check all the boxes and you have made your decision about where to rent a place, it's now time to "seal the deal" with your landlord. You'll need to sign a lease which is a written rental agreement or contract that outlines all the terms and conditions that both of you agreed to. Make sure that you understand everything written on it before you sign as it is a legal document, and can be used against you if problems arise. Here are the things that usually appear in a rental lease in Canada:

o Your landlord's complete names and contact details

o The address of the place your renting out

o The cost of the monthly rent you have agreed to, this will include other things like utilities, furniture, services, parking, and other amenities.

o The due date for the rental payment including the amount of how much the rent can increase in the future

o Term of rental period (6 months to 1 year contract; month per month etc.)

o Terms when cancelling, subletting, or ending your lease

o Restrictions within the property/unit building

o Other rules that your landlord have listed (if any)

o Procedures if there'll be any disagreements, lease changes or landlord/tenant issues.

o Rental deposit agreements (usually the deposit is the cost of one month's rent); will vary from city to city. In Quebec, landlords are not allowed to ask for deposits.

Acquiring a House and Lot in Canada

Let me break a common notion for you, a house in NOT an investment. It is however, an asset. Though, your house will not make any money for you unless you rent it out to someone or you sell it. In my opinion, a house is more of a liability than an asset. This is because even after you paid it in full, the expenses won't stop as you'll still need to pay for real estate taxes (the bigger the property, the larger the tax), for maintenance/repairs/renovations/utilities, for housing insurances, and on top of that the headaches you'll need to go through when acquiring/ paying a property. There's no return of investment for a long time unless of course you sell it at a higher price or let somebody lease it/ turn it into a rental business.

There are lots of factors you need to think about when buying a house. One of the first things you need to consider is purchasing a property you can afford, and how much it will appreciate over time.

There are lots of good real estate agents in Canada that will help you out when buying a home. You just need to make sure that the agent/agency is trustworthy, and someone who will listen to your needs. You can ask for recommendations from different sources like your family, friends, online forums/expat groups, and also recommendations from immigration organizations in Canada. You can also visit the Multiple Listing Services website at www.mls.ca for lists of recommended real estate agents, and homes that are up for sale. Of course, the best way is to still drive around your chosen neighborhood and see which houses that are for sale will attract you.

Making an Offer

After finding a house that fits your taste, budget, lifestyle, and family, you can now make a purchase offer. If you have a real estate agent, he/she will help you prepare an offer. If you don't have one, then you might need a lawyer to help you prepare this document. If your offer is accepted, and the terms of payment is already in place as agreed by you and the owner of the property, you'll then need to hire a lawyer to transfer the property rights to your name.

Financing Options for Homes in Canada

Most homebuyers will need the aid of a bank or a financial institution when purchasing houses. People will get a housing loan (or a mortgage) from a bank/financial institution so that they can acquire and live in their house with a promise of paying it back through regular payments over a period of time (usually around 25 years – maximum). Of course, there'll be interest charges.

It's best to also get a mortgage pre – approval with the help of a mortgage broker or someone from the bank so that your needs can be tailored to your financial capacity, and you'll know how much you'll spend for your home.

In Canada, when it comes to availing a housing loan from a bank or any financial institution one of the first things they do is check the borrower's credit history. This will help the lender determine if you are doing your due diligence, your loan application for your house will have a higher/faster rate of approval if you have a good track record of paying previous loans.

If you're a newcomer immigrant, obviously you won't have any prior credit history; if this is the case then it's highly recommended that you ask the help of your chosen bank's customer representative so that they can help develop a plan on how you can create a good credit history because this is one of the major requirements of Canadian banks when purchasing a home or acquiring mortgage.

Other Housing Options in Canada

Government – Subsidized Housing

The government of Canada helps people with low incomes acquires a house through subsidy. This is where the government pays a portion of the rents so that low income earners can afford to have a home or be able to rent out apartments. Rules and regulations vary from one province to another, and the process is quite daunting especially if you're an immigrant or a refugee. You won't be given priority, and will most likely be on the waiting list for many years. What most immigrants do while waiting for the government to subsidize their homes is to live temporarily in private rental housing, and tries to get higher income jobs so that they can afford accommodation costs.

Co-op/ Cooperative Housing

This is where members of a cooperative collectively owned and manage apartments or houses where they live. Most cooperative organizations are not for profit which is why rents are way cheaper than the average. However, you need to become a member first, and be able to actively participate with the organization or the maintenance of the houses. You should submit an application to the governing body of the cooperative where you want to live. Once you get accepted, you'll need to sign an occupancy agreement which is similar to signing a lease.

Student Housing

Canada also offers many housing options for foreign students who will stay in the country for the duration of their studies. If you're a student immigrant, you can check out information regarding the on – campus and off – campus options that are available in many universities and colleges in each province.

Housing for Seniors

Canada offers many housing options for seniors (both locals and properly documented immigrants). Such residences are usually funded by the government, and it also comes with various services to help senior in their everyday needs.

Estate Planning

Estate planning involves making a written will. A will that is properly signed and witnessed is very important because it gives the piece of paper the power to legally pass the property or titles to the rightful heirs once the owner dies.

If you're an expat or someone who bought a house or property in Canada, it's highly recommended that you create a written will to ensure that the properties you bought and worked hard for will go to the right person/s, and will go through an easy legal process.

The main function of estate plans is to properly and smoothly distribute your property or properties whether it is a land, and/or a house and lot to your children or chosen heirs when you pass away. Many people or families are familiar with their estate plans but most people are not, and this is why problems arise. Many only availed a one – size – fits – all plan, and not even bothered in seeking any legal professional to customize their chosen plans in order to meet their needs and/or wishes.

Tips When Making a Will

- Your estate should include your assets (properties/lands you own), and your liabilities (what you owe, either your mortgage, other estate loans etc.)

- Provinces and territories in Canada have their owne set of estate laws so make sure that you're aware of it when finalizing your will.

- It's important to keep your will up to date (especially if you are continuously acquiring properties, have been paying up your mortgage, or recently getting another mortgage) because it will help your estate lawyer/representative when you die.

- Creating a will is actually optional; you are not required by the law to prepare one. However, if you die without a will, the estate laws in the province, city or territory where your property is located will take effect. This means that your local government will be the one to decide how your estate will be divided in accordance with the current laws in place.

- It's highly recommended that you hire an estate lawyer or get professional help when making a will so that these experts can guide you and help you properly with the documents, legal matters, witnesses, and legal fees involved.

- In Canada, some provinces or territories cancel previous wills made if the owner is about to get married, divorced, or living with a common – law partner.

- You can also have the option of naming an estate representative. This is the person who will manage your estate after you die. They are also known as the executor, liquidator, and estate trustee. You can have the option of choosing more than one, and these people will need to follow the instructions/requests you have written in your will. Make sure that your estate representative knows his/her responsibilities so that everything is in place just in case!

- If you didn't name any estate representative, the courts in your province or territory will assign someone to manage your properties.

Chapter Five: Utilities and Communication Services in Canada

In Canada primary utilities like electricity, water, and gas are usually included in the residence or rental house. You'll just have to sign papers or go directly to the office of providers in the area so that you can properly set up an account. You'll need to fill up forms and provide your personal details, credit card number, and other necessary documents as well as your credit history. If you don't have a credit history yet since you're a newcomer, the providers in Canada usually requires the customer to either pay an advance deposit or get a co –signer to guarantee your account.

It's best that you inform your provider at least a week or two before you moved in your new home so that it'll be up and running. If you're renting, the utilities and connections are usually bundled, and a collective bill will be issued to you every month. Just make sure to clarify it with your landlord, and ask him/her about your payment options.

This chapter will provide you with general information about how to set up the needed housing utilities. We'll also give you an overview of the different mobile and internet plans that are available in the country so that you can make a comparative review of each.

Housing Utilities

Electricity

Most provinces and territories in Canada have their own electric providers. The electric company in your chosen areas is in charge of generating electricity, transmission, and distribution of electric power to the entire province. Canada's electric voltage is 110 to 120 Volts (60 hertz), and the outlets require 3 – pronged North American Ground plugs.

If you're renting out the electricity is most likely metered separately at the discretion of the co – owners or the landlord. Make sure to ask your landlord about it or go directly to the service provider to clarify the consumption and billing policies. Depending on your provider, bills are usually issued monthly, bi – monthly or quarterly. Some providers will need security deposits from you which can be paid in cash or cheque. After demonstrating 1 year of good payment track record, your security deposit will be returned with interest. For an average household electricity usually costs about CAD$80 to $130 per month.

Gas

Gas services are being provided by the local gas establishments around your area, and most providers in Canada are natural gas distributors. It comes with a credit meter to measure consumption. After the meter readings, the bills will be sent to your house.

Of course the monthly costs will depend on how much you consume. For an average household, people pay around CAD$75 - $95. For those being supplied with natural gas, you only have 2 weeks to pay for your gas bills otherwise there'll be an additional payment charges if you're late.

Water

The quality of water in almost all of the provinces in Canada is excellent. Water usage here are relatively higher compared to Europe because the water tariffs are lower. Water utilities are commonly bundled if you're renting out a property. The great advantage of people who rent is that they're not in charge of setting up a water service or maintaining it.

If you happen to consume more than the allowable water rate per month, it will be added to your bill after the initial meter reading. The usual cost per cubic meter is CAD$0.22. Your monthly bill will again depend on your consumption.

Mobile Plans in Canada

Canada uses a standard GSM and CDMA system depending on your location. For expats, you can still bring your mobile phones from your home country but there's a big chance that it will not be supported by your potential provider in Canada. You can ask your local provider if they are partners with any of the telecommunication providers in Canada.

When choosing a mobile service provider, make sure to inquire about the length of the contracts in the mobile/ service plans you'll choose so that you can change your options if need be, and you won't be locked into a contract.

The average mobile plan in Canada per month will costs anywhere between CAD$35 – CAD$60. We've compiled the leading Canadian mobile providers and their best plans in this section. This is also an advantage for you to compare prices, features, and package deals so that you'll know what best suits you and your needs. The leading mobile services and mobile plan providers in Canada are Rogers, Telus, and Bell.

Rogers

- **Best Mobile Plan Base Rate:** CAD$60/month
- **Data:** 500 Megabytes
- **Canada – wide calling additional rate:** CAD$10/month

- **USA and North American calls additional rate:** CAD$25/month

- **For iPhone 5 (3 year contract):** $299

- **Samsung Galaxy 4:** for 3 year contract, the upfront payment is CAD$299; for 1 year contract – CAD$699

- **Activation fee:** $35

Features:

- Includes 1,000 local daytime mins.

- Unlimited texts and calls starting 6 P.M. on local evenings and weekends, including unlimited caller ID and voice mails.

Telus

- **Best Mobile Plan Base Rate:** CAD$60/month

- **Data:** 500 Megabytes

- **Canada – wide calling additional rate:** CAD50 cents/minute

- **USA calls additional rate (per 30 minutes):** CAD$3/month

- **USA calls additional rate (without add - on):** CAD$1.50/minute

- **For iPhone 5 (3 year contract):** $179

- **Samsung Galaxy 4:** for a 3 year contract, the upfront payment is CAD$199;

- **Activation fee:** none but you'll need a sim card which costs CAD$10

Features:

- Includes 1,000 local daytime mins.

- Unlimited texts and calls starting 6 P.M. on local evenings and weekends, including unlimited video and picture messaging.

- Telus won't charge any shipping fees for your device, and you are entitled to a 30 – day trial period to use the mobile device. You can send it back if you don't like it without any additional delivery charges.

Bell

- **Best Mobile Plan Base Rate:** CAD$50/month

- **Data:** 150 Megabytes with unlimited Wi - Fi

- **Canada – wide calling additional rate:** CAD50 cents/minute

- **USA calls additional rate (without add - on):** CAD50 cents/minute

- **For iPhone 5 (3 year contract):** $179.95; for month to month contract payment of CAD$700 up front.

- **Samsung Galaxy 4:** for 3 year contract, the upfront payment is CAD$199.95; for month to month contract payment of CAD$700 up front.

- **Activation fee:** can be waived

Features:

- Includes 1,000 local daytime mins.

- Unlimited texts and calls starting 6 P.M. on local evenings and weekends, including unlimited caller ID, voice mails, conference calls, voice and picture messaging, call waiting

Internet Plans and Providers in Canada

There are many internet service providers in the whole country, and you also have various internet plan options that ranges from CAD$30 - CAD$250 depending on your monthly usage. You can also choose from dial – up and broadband services. Usually unlimited plans with fast mbps or large bandwidths are more expensive. The quality of internet connection in all of Canada is fast and efficient.

This section will give you an overview of the different internet services providers and their various internet plans together with the speed data, monthly consumption cap and cost per month. We'll also give you the best features of each service providers.

Shaw

Features for all internet plans:

- Includes Wi – Fi modem (for rental)
- Includes TV and movie streaming services
- Includes McAfee internet security program/ anti – virus programs

- Includes Shaw Go Wi – Fi which allows you to connect on multiple devices with up to 30 Mbps all over Canada

- Technical support availability 24/7 through phone, email, and online chat

Plans

- Internet 5
    - $60/month
    - Download Speed: 5 Mbps
    - Upload Speed: 1 Mbps
    - Usage cap per month: 65 GB

- Internet 15
    - $70/month
    - Download Speed: 15 Mbps
    - Upload Speed: 1.5 Mbps
    - Usage cap per month: 150 GB

- Internet 75

  - $80/month

  - Download Speed: 75 Mbps

  - Upload Speed: 7.5 Mbps

  - Usage cap per month: 500 GB

- Internet 150

  - $105/month

  - Download Speed: 150 Mbps

  - Upload Speed: 15 Mbps

  - Usage cap per month: Unlimited

Telus

Features for all internet plans:

- You can save $5 off in all rates when you bundle it with TV, mobile, and phone plans
- Includes Norton internet security program/ anti – virus programs (for 2 devices with plans)
- Technical support availability 24/7 through phone, email, and online chat

Plans

- Internet 15

    o $68/month

    o Download Speed: 15 Mbps

    o Upload Speed: 1 Mbps

    o Usage cap per month: 200 GB

- Internet 25

    o $73/month

    o Download Speed: 25 Mbps

    o Upload Speed: 5 Mbps

    o Usage cap per month: 300 GB

- Internet 50

    o $77/month

    o Download Speed: 50 Mbps

    o Upload Speed: 10 Mbps

    o Usage cap per month: 450 GB

- Internet 150

    o $82/month

    o Download Speed: 150 Mbps

- o Upload Speed: 150 Mbps

- o Usage cap per month: 1 Terabyte

Bell

Features for all internet plans:

- One – time activation fee for only $49.95

- Includes modem rental

- Includes McAfee internet security program/ anti – virus programs (for 2 devices with plans)

- Unlimited date usage when bundled with TV for an extra $10/month.

- Technical support availability 24/7 through phone, email, and online chat

Plans

- Essential Plus

  - o $29.95/month

  - o Download Speed: 3 Mbps

  - o Upload Speed: 0.68 Mbps

  - o Usage cap per month: 20 GB

- Fibre 25

    o $74.95/month

    o Download Speed: 25 Mbps

    o Upload Speed: 10 Mbps

    o Usage cap per month: 350 GB

- Fibre 50

    o $89.95/month

    o Download Speed: 50 Mbps

    o Upload Speed: 10 Mbps

    o Usage cap per month: Unlimited

- Fibre 100

    o $94.95/month

    o Download Speed: 100 Mbps

    o Upload Speed: 10 Mbps

    o Usage cap per month: Unlimited

- Fibre 150

    o $99.95/month

    o Download Speed: 150 Mbps

    o Upload Speed: 50 Mbps

    o Usage cap per month: Unlimited

- Fibre 300

    o $109.95/month

    o Download Speed: 300 Mbps

    o Upload Speed: 100 Mbps

    o Usage cap per month: Unlimited

- Gigabit Fibre

    o $149.95/month

    o Download Speed: 1 Gbps

    o Upload Speed: 100 Mbps

    o Usage cap per month: Unlimited

Rogers

Features for all internet plans:

- Installation fee for only $49.99 (waived if self – installed)

- Activation fee costs $14.95

- Includes modem rental

- Includes Rogers Online Protection Basic internet security program/ anti – virus programs (for 2 devices with plans)

- Includes Easy Connect Software

- Technical support availability 24/7 through phone, email, and online chat

Plans

- Internet 5

  o $32.99/month

  o Download Speed: 5 Mbps

  o Upload Speed: 1 Mbps

  o Usage cap per month: 25 GB

- Rogers Ignite 30

  o $69.99/month

  o Download Speed: 30 Mbps

  o Upload Speed: 5 Mbps

  o Usage cap per month: 250 GB

- Rogers Ignite 75

  o $84.99/month

  o Download Speed: 75 Mbps

  o Upload Speed: 10 Mbps

- o Usage cap per month: 500 GB

- Rogers Ignite 150ou
  - o $99.99/month
  - o Download Speed: 150 Mbps
  - o Upload Speed: 15 Mbps
  - o Usage cap per month: Unlimited

- Rogers Ignite 500ou
  - o $119.99/month
  - o Download Speed: 500 Mbps
  - o Upload Speed: 20 Mbps
  - o Usage cap per month: Unlimited

- Rogers Ignite Gigabit
  - o $144.99/month
  - o Download Speed: 1 Gbps
  - o Upload Speed: 30 Mbps
  - o Usage cap per month: Unlimited

Chapter Six: Work and Business in Canada

Finding a job or setting up a business is what most expats do after relocating in Canada. After all, everyone needs a source of income, unless of course, you're already retired wherein you're just going to depend on your pension or prior investments, or unless someone will support you during your stay. But if you're not a retired person or dependent on anyone, then finding a job and building a business should be your main priority after getting all the permits/ visa you need or after you and your family have settled down.

For many expats, landing a job is quite challenging because the application process can be different from one's home country, but perhaps it's much harder to land a work that will match your qualifications, interests, and financial needs. This is certainly a big challenge for any newcomer who is still adjusting to the expat life in Canada because it will take some time (and perhaps many unwanted jobs) before you can build your working qualifications and gain a working experience in the country that will hopefully attract the job you want.

This chapter will also cover how an expat like you can set up your own business, the permits you need to have, and the process of registering your business. This will all be essential to ensure that you won't break any laws regarding earning money and making a living in Canada.

Working in Canada

Expats who wish to get a job in Canada will need either a residence permit (permanent residency visa) or a temporary working permit. Many foreigners are being approved every year but it's important to note that the requirements and eligibility will certainly differ between the two.

Aside from getting these working permits, you'll also need to have a Social Insurance Number issued by the Canadian government through an organization called Service Canada so that you'll be entitled to many employee benefits.

Residence Permits

As mentioned in the immigration chapter of this book, residence permits/visas are for those foreigners who wanted to stay in Canada to live and work on a long – term basis or permanently. If you are granted a permanent residency permit/visa, you're not just entitled to work in Canada but you are also eligible to the country's social system, various immigrant benefits such as education, and healthcare. Resident visa holders include the right to live in the country for a long – term basis, and also have the option to become a naturalized Canadian citizen.

You'll also be entitled to various political, economic, social, and environmental rights to name a few. Go back to the immigration chapter of this book to know which visa program will cater to you in terms of working in Canada or inquire in your nearest Canadian embassy on how you can apply for a temporary working permit, and eventually transition to acquiring a residency permit/visa as this is one common way of how expats get to stay in the country for the long – term.

Temporary Work Permits

If you're a foreigner whose only purpose is to complete a job for a Canadian/international employer, or to simply work here and take advantage of the many job opportunities but do not intend to live in Canada for good, then you will just need a temporary working permit. Once you're granted with this kind of work permit, it only means that you're legally in the country for work purposes but you are not entitled to any Canadian rights, and is only allowed to stay in the country for a certain period of time as such permits have an expiration date. You may need to get another one or apply for an extension if your employer in Canada will renew your contract.

Usually work permits are applied before you go to Canada but of course there are some exceptions to this rule. For example, citizens of United States, United Kingdom, New Zealand, Australia, and other European countries will need not just a temporary working permit but also apply for a temporary residence visa before they can settle in Canada. Check the website of the Canadian government at www.cic.ga.ca to know if your country is included with those who must apply for the second document.

How to Apply for a Temporary Working Permit

Before being granted a temporary working permit by the immigration of Canada, you'll need to first secure a job offer from a Canadian company, business, government, or employer. You should also be able to prove that the job you're applying for or have been accepted to, is something that cannot be filled with a Canadian/local employee. This is because Canadian citizens and those who already obtained a permanent resident status are the government's top priority in terms of filling job opportunities. If you are applying as a skilled worker, then you must prove that you just don't have the skills but also the experience to assume the job so that your application will have a greater chance of being approved.

Here are the steps on how you can apply for a temporary working permit in Canada:

- **Secure a job offer/ contract from the Canadian employer you applied to.** Ideally, the offer should state the position in which you are accepted, the name of the company/employer, nature of the job, company address, duration of the job/contract, and other important details. A confirmation letter that you were accepted in the company and in a particular position will also do.

- **Your employer should have obtained the Positive Labor Market Opinion.** This is a written confirmation from the Human Resources and Social Development

Canada department. Basically, this only means that your potential employer has already posted an advertisement for the position throughout Canada for about 3 months already.

- **Once you have both documents mentioned above, you can now submit a temporary working permit application** to a Canadian Visa Office at www.cic.gc.ca.Make sure to always check this website and stay updated because the requirements are subject to change.

- **You should also prepare supplemental documents** like your birth certificate, IDs, qualification certificates, diplomas, transcripts, police clearance, medical certificates to prove that you're healthy and able to carry out the job, references from previous employers and other necessary documents that will be required from you.

- **Get ready for a one – on – one interview.** Once the Canadian Visa Office received your application, you will most likely be scheduled for an interview appointment. Aside from your personal background, the interview will be about your previous working experience, the educational levels you have attained, or the skills you have acquired to confirm that you are a certified skilled/professional worker.

- **Just wait and keep the faith.** The duration of your application will vary as it will undergo through a thorough review by the Canadian Visa Office. On average though, it takes about 1 to 3 months before being approved. You'll also most likely pay for an application fee, keep tab on that as prices can also change without prior notice.

Regulated Occupations in Canada

Many professions in Canada have set its own standards for how such work is practiced, they call it regulated occupations. There are about 20% of jobs that are regulated by the provincial/territorial government as granted by the legislation. This means that the local government has the authority to regulate certain jobs in order to ensure that the workers meet the standards of practice, and that they are competent for the job. Such organizations also aim to protect the public and keep them safe by ensuring that such professions are always align with the governments regulations.

If you wanted to work in a regulated occupation you should be a licensed or a certified professional/worker. Another way is to register to an organization in the province or territory where you work, and that this bodies regulates occupation. The most common examples of regulated occupations are in the fields of legal services, law, government, healthcare, engineering, and finance. A person who has a regulated occupation must have taken examinations, must have been evaluated in terms of their communication/language skills, and have also gained working experience over a period of time. The requirements will vary from one province/territory to another.

Unregulated Occupations in Canada

Unregulated occupations are jobs that don't need a license, certificate or a registration from a governing body/institution.

Most jobs in the country are in the category of non – regulated occupations. Of course, the requirements for employment will vary but as an applicant, you should ensure that you have the education, experience, and passion to perform the job properly.

For those who are applying to be a skilled worker, you should be able to show that you have a certain level of competence, have gained necessary education for the job, and also have the right personal qualities.

If you are applying as a professional, say a job in marketing, you don't need to acquire a certification of some sort, but your employer will expect you to have completed a degree in business or related courses, and have also acquired certain amount of training/experience in the field of marketing. Usually, your employer will be the one to determine if the qualifications you gained from your previous job experiences or the education you attained is equivalent to their Canadian standards.

How to Search for Jobs

Since you're a newcomer, it's given that you have no idea where to start looking for work, and is most likely not yet familiar with regards to how the 'job – hunting system' works in Canada, don't worry because this section will guide you where you can start your search for that 'dream job' you always wanted!

There are many places to search for jobs in Canada both for a short – term work and for the long – term. Below are some of the best places where you can start your search:

- If you are eyeing to apply at a certain Canadian company or if you're looking to apply for a certain position, then it's best that you go directly to the company's website and check if there are any posts of job vacancies. This is also a great way for you to check the background of the company, and see if this is where you want to work for in the future. You'll also get to have an idea about what kind of employees or professionals they're looking for.

- The next thing is to search jobs through various job search websites. Now, there are many out there, both local and international websites. Before giving out your information or applying to a certain job post, make sure that the company is legit and is existing. Established companies and businesses usually have websites, social media pages, and telephone numbers or better yet go directly to their office to confirm if they have an opening (provided that the company address is listed). If none of these details are given, better not apply in these kinds of job posts, just to be safe. We'd like to recommend that you start searching through Service Canada's website at www.jobbank.gc.ca. They have a large job database, and it also links to other job search websites. Since this is a government related website, you can be quite sure that the jobs posted here are legit.

- You can always do it the old fashioned way by checking out job ads from the newspaper, your community centers, local government offices, and immigrant - serving organizations. Why not directly call the company you're planning to apply in, and ask if they have any job vacancies. Sometimes, companies are not directly advertising because they rely on recommendations, and walk – in applicants.

- Attend job fairs. Canada provides job fairs every now and then in particular cities, towns, and areas. This is another great place to reach out to your potential employers because if a certain company/employer is included in this job fair that means they are looking to hire employees and are open to discussing job opportunities. Make sure that your CV (Curriculum Vitae) or resume, cover letter, and other qualification documents are always ready. Dress up nicely, and always be ready for an on – the – spot job interview. Remember, first impressions last.

- Another option is to use an employment agency which will do the job searching for you in a way. These agencies will act as a third party between you and your potential employer. You can visit www.jobsetc.gc.ca for government employment services or go to a Service Canada center near you for assistance.

- Network with the locals around your area or in your province, and ask for referrals/recommendations from your friends and family. As the old saying goes, it's not what you know, it's who you know. Do not get discouraged if at first you don't succeed, like everything else in life, timing is everything. Just be patient, keep looking, keep applying, and never give up!

Doing Business in Canada

In terms of the ease in setting up a business, Canada is in the top 19 countries in the world (out of 189) which means that the country is a favorable place to establish a start – up and run a business. There are many foreign nationals who started their own business in the Maple Country, and had been successful about it, and there are also others who set – up branches of their existing business to reach a larger market. Similar before you find a job in Canada, it's important that you are well – documented before you set – up a business or a company.

Make sure that you are a permanent resident in the country or you're a naturalized Canadian citizen so that you'd have the legal right once the government checks up on you/your business. The Canadian government created various visa programs to accommodate the needs of foreign nationals wishing to stay, work, and/or do business in the country. Recently, they created a visa program targeted for entrepreneurs called the Start – Up Visa Program.

This aims to help those who wanted to start a business in Canada, and it also speeds up the immigration process for entrepreneurs looking to become permanent residents in the country because if you have complied with the requirements, and you have proven that your business can contribute in Canada's economy one way or another, your permanent residency visa can be granted within just a few weeks.

Of course, creating a start – up business or even establishing another branch is not that easy, and doing all of this so that you can be granted a permanent visa is also quite complicated. Basically, for an entrepreneur to be eligible under the start – up visa program, one will need financial backing from investors that are designated by the Canadian government; one will also need to prepare a business plan, along with other documents/evidences proving that your business will work in the Canadian marketplace. This is not an easy road for any entrepreneur but it is something worth taking especially if you intend to live in Canada for good. This is a win – win for you as an expat entrepreneur, for Canada's economy, and for your business as it will reach a wider market.

Types of Legal Structures for Business in Canada

Assuming that you already acquired a permanent residency visa or you have been qualified under the Startup Visa Program, the next thing you should think about it the kind of legal structure that will be best suited for your company/business as it will determine your financial, legal and also tax obligations. There are 3 common types of legal structures for businesses in Canada; these are sole proprietorship/self – employed, partnership, and LLC (Limited Liability Company).

Sole Proprietor

Perhaps the main advantage of setting up a sole proprietorship is that you are in full control and ownership of your business. This is the kind of legal structure best suited for self – employed expats. Another advantage is that the after – tax profit of the company all goes to the owner. Setting up a sole proprietorship is also simple, much quicker, and cheaper compared to registering under a partnership or an LLC.

Of course, the downside is that you are the only one liable for the losses/failures of your business and you'll be in charge of almost everything – the operation, the management, the accounting, the records, and everything in between. You're basically a one man team here which can also be quite challenging especially if you're starting a business from scratch.

Partnership

If you have 2 or more business partners or co – owners, then the legal structure for your company is a partnership. When you set up and register your business, you and your partners should have a written agreement about the rights and duties of one another. All of your partners should be aware if there will be any changes to the agreement, and you'll need to also have a company lawyer. The agreement must stipulate if the partners have equal rights in the company as some may have invested more than others or have put up more capital during the start - up.

The largest shareholder will likely have more rights in the company, but all partners are still jointly responsible for all the obligations and potential losses incurred. Each partner should pay their own income taxes depending on the amount of their shared profits.

Limited Liability Corporation (LLC)

An LLC is an alternative if you or your partners don't want to have a standard partnership kind of legal structure for your company. This is pretty much the same with standard partnerships in all respects, the only difference is that the partners have limited liabilities to pay the debts incurred by other partner/s.

Incorporation

Incorporation is usually for big shot companies/businesses that have large capitals, huge market range, have board of investors, and companies that already has a certain reputation and credibility in the business world. The rules of incorporation vary from one province to another, and it will usually take a longer time to set up.

The process of incorporation is quite tedious as there would be a lot of documents and proofs needed, and it will also require the services of a corporate lawyer/s.

How to Set Up a Business in Canada

Once you have decided which legal structure to take, it's now time to register your company or business. The process and requirements will vary from one province/territory to another so it's best that you check with your local government for updates regarding these. You can also register your business federally especially you'd be establishing it across the country (ex: branches). Here is the overview of how to set up your business/company:

Step #1: Choose a unique business name. You'll need to make sure that your company's business name is not identical to any existing business, and was never used before. You can do this by searching in business registration databases.

Step #2: Once you've registered a business name, and it's approved, your business will now be assigned with a business number (BN) or a Quebec Enterprise Number (NEQ) for those residing in the area.

Step #3: You will then be required to submit all necessary documents both from you/ your partners, and your business docs/ records along with other supplemental documents. Again, the requirements will vary depending on the kind of legal structure you chose, and the province your business/company is registered at.

Step #4: You'll need to also draft written agreements (for partnerships/LLC/incorporation) with the presence of a lawyer, and all your business partners as this will also be submitted along with your business documents.

Step #5: Once you've completed all the necessary steps that your province will require, and once you already know your tax and other obligations, your business will be granted with an approval, and you'll be given the official documents for your company as it will be now deemed legit.

Chapter Seven: Family & Education in Canada

Canada is committed to strengthening family bonds for foreign nationals, and this is very evident through their many visa programs that are targeted for expats with families. The main applicant can apply for a resident visa, and also have the opportunity to bring their immediate families including their spouses/common – law partner, children, parents, grandparents, and other relatives that are eligible under the Family Sponsorship Class Visa.

The Canadian government has also been approving thousands of applications more than ever particularly for expats intending to become a permanent resident in the country together with their families because they want to open more opportunities for people, and because they believe that foreign families can contribute to the robust and growing economy of the country.

There are many opportunities and unique Canadian experiences awaiting foreign expats and their families, not to mention the many benefits that permanent residents can take advantage of such as the quality of education, various healthcare benefits, tax breaks, as well as employment and business opportunities. According to various surveys conducted over the past few years, the quality of life is what many immigrants like about relocating in Canada. Various social, economic, environmental, political, and cultural factors contribute in making Canada one of the top places in the world to raise families.

Acclimating Children Once You Make the Move

Coming to Canada opens many doors especially for immigrant children particularly in the education sector because Canada has one of the top educational systems in the world. However, one of the main concerns of immigrant parents is the many adjustments that their children need to make once they make the move. Acclimating children can be tough socially and culturally for some especially for young kids and teenagers as they have already gotten used to the way of living in their home country.

Immigrant children are usually more pressured socially and culturally because they need to have a sort of balance between maintaining their traditional values/customs, and conforming to Canadian practices. It can also be quite harder especially if you're settling in places like Quebec since they would need to learn the French language and also the French customs which could cause culture shock especially for non – Europeans. Sometimes the children can also suffer from prejudice, and discrimination particularly for minorities.

These can affect one's self – confidence, attitude, social relationships, and also damage family relationships, which is why it's important that parents' guide their children during the transition process, and constantly check up on them about their personal lives, and social lives.

It's also best that you immerse you children within the community by getting to know the locals around your neighborhood, attending parties as a family, and also being there for them during various social/school activities. It won't be a surprise if your children act out at first, but your support and understanding is the key in making sure that their emotional needs are being met.

Another way of acclimating your children in Canada is to regularly do family trips with them. As you may now have known there are lots of amazing places in the country that are perfect for families. Canada is a place where families can truly bond with one another through various outdoor activities which is why it's highly recommended that one of the first things you should do is to let them explore the place, go on hikes, go do water – related activities or just simply gather 'round for picnics every now and then, so that you can spent quality time with them, and face the new life together.

Living in Canada

Canada is the 2nd best country to live in both for locals and immigrants (with Germany being the first), according to a study done by the World Economic Forum. That's great news if you're planning to move here with your wife and kids for good because the quality of life here is truly impeccable. Canadians are also friendly and welcoming people, and their cultural environment is quite vibrant despite of the 'cold ambience.'

Canada makes it the best choice for expat families as their new home bur there are still many things to consider and factors to weigh in if you're planning to move to Canada with your whole family.

Aside from finding the best school for your kids, you also need to factor in your daily financial and logistical needs as well as family – friendly services, not to mention, the healthcare and safety concerns for your family. This section will focus on some important factors on why Canada is one of the top residential choices of expat families.

Whatever kind of living environment you choose, the pace of life you want to experience, the cuisines you wanted to taste, the kind of education you want your children to have, and the comfortable life you dream of having, there's always something for everyone here in the icy cold country of the north!

The World Economic Forum ranked Canada as one of the top family – friendly countries in the world because of the following factors:

- **Safety:** Canada is perhaps the safest country in the world (and pretty much throughout history) which makes it the best place to raise children without making the parents paranoid about unexpected violent attacks or even petty crimes. Being the safest country means that, Canadians in general are well – disciplined people and the law enforcement in the country is quite impeccable. The crime rates are very low in most provinces/ cities and territories. Expect to have a very peaceful lifestyle once you and your family make the move.

- **Political and Economic Stability:** Canada is part of the G7 (Group of 7) which is an international organization of the top 7 largest and most stable economies in the world. Canada's government is a combination of parliamentary democracy, and constitutional monarchy. And it's robust and resilient economy is what makes it more suitable for foreign nationals who are looking to make a living here for their families. The Canadian government is also lauded as having one of the most effective political systems in the world. According to worldwide statistics, Canada's government has 97% rate in effectiveness. Canada truly cares for the welfare of its citizen.

- **Cost of Living:** The cost of living in Canada is quite pricey so to speak but it's because the quality of living here is impeccable in all respects across the country.

Compared to United States, the costs of goods and services in the Maple Country are much cheaper. However, the housing costs in some cities like Toronto and Vancouver is definitely more expensive compared to other Canadian cities, though it should also be noted that the average household income in the two cities are also way higher.

- **Job Opportunities:** Raising a family means that one should be able to support it financially, which means that finding a job is one of the top priorities for expats in Canada. The good news is that Canada's job market is not as saturated compared to other countries like the United States. The country is always looking for ways to increase job opportunities not just for its locals citizens but also for incoming immigrants. Most employment opportunities are found in the manufacturing, and natural resource sectors which means that skilled workers are very much in – demand in the country. There are also lots of jobs targeted for professionals or those who wish to work in the corporate world. Doing business in Canada can also be done with ease, making everyone have the equal opportunity to take advantage of the Canadian market, and also ride its growing economy.

- **Family – Friendly and Welcoming Attitude for Expats:** Different factors like safety, healthcare, environmentally friendly atmosphere, great landmarks, diversity, schools, and favorable economy, Canada is generally a country built by foreigners. It is one of the nations who welcome diversity, cultural differences, and immigrants with open arms. You and your children will surely be able to adjust in no time because the local communities in each provinces/cities are very supportive to expats.

- **Healthcare:** Canada's healthcare policies are also top – notched. The government has allotted huge funds to keep improving its citizen's public health and medical insurance systems. Your parents or grandparents who might be ill can take advantage of the great healthcare system in place as long as you/ your family are eligible or have legal rights to be in Canada. The government usually covers different healthcare services in public hospitals and accredited medical clinics but depending on your immigration status some restrictions apply. You can also get additional coverage once you get employed. The Medicare system in Canada is available across the whole country, and each province also has its own medical services even if you don't yet have a health card.

- **Educational System:** Canada is also one of the leading countries when it comes to education. In fact, according to a report, immigrant students perform very well regardless of their social or ethnic backgrounds. The country boasts its public and private universities, learning systems, and its various scholarship opportunities. Students can study part – time and full – time, and also have opportunities for those who are disabled and children coming from low – income families.

School Options and Education Systems in Canada

In Canada, there's no such thing as a national system of education because each province and territory has its own, although the educational system or curriculum is very similar, there are still some variations depending on the place as well as the particular school/university where you or your child is studying. For example, in some places, there's only one department of education, and in other provinces there are two (one for elementary/secondary education, and for post – secondary/college education.

This is section will provide you with an overview of the many aspects of the Canadian education system, and the general things you need to know regarding enrollment, credentials, and other academic – related information to help you or your children get started, and have a basic idea of how the education system works in this country.

Elementary and Secondary Education

For those expats who have children that are still under the basic level of education (elementary and secondary/ middle – school/high school) will have to complete a total of 12 years in order to become eligible for post – secondary or college education.

Primary education for kids begins at kindergarten, followed by grades 1 to 12 (elementary is from grades 1 to 6; secondary/high school is from grades 7 to 12 in most provinces/territories). Once the student completes secondary school, he/she will receive a high school diploma, and be eligible for post – secondary education.

The school year begins at the last week of August, and ends around the last week of June. If your children arrive in Canada in the middle of the school year, and you wish for your child to go ahead and study, then it's best that you contact the school board regarding this matter. It'll be up to them if your child can still catch up and attend the rest of the school year (if it's not too late) otherwise you'll just have to wait until the next school year starts.

The elementary and post – secondary education in Canada is funded by the Canadian government through the taxes from its citizens. The government funded schools are mostly public schools but there are also lots of private schools in the country though it's not for free. There could also be some requirements that may apply for expat children like the residence requirements to see if your kids are eligible to get a free education.

As designated by the law, children whose aged 5 or 6 should attend school up until they finish secondary education or until they reach the age of around 16 to 18 years old. Parents can also have the option to home – school their kids.

Secondary Education for Adults

If you're an expat who wished to continue your high school education because you have not completed your primary education, you can have the option to choose from many adult education programs that are available depending on your province or territory. There are classes that teach literacy programs, and you can also take up subjects that will lead to a high school diploma provided that you are eligible or have had some sort of credentials from your previous schooling in your home country or wherever you studied. Make sure to inquire about this in the school board of the institution you intend to study at.

Post – Secondary or College Education

There are various types of college institutions and forms of post – secondary educations in the country; most of which are recognized by the Canadian government because these schools and the programs they are offering have met the government's educational standards. This means that such schools or universities are given an authority to grant diplomas, certifications, bachelor degrees, and other qualifications.

There are also institutions that are not officially recognized because they didn't undergo government quality control or have not yet pass certain educational standards.

Generally, college education in Canada makes up for 2 semesters in one school year; the first term starts from September to December, and the second term starts in January to April. Summer break is from May to August, but universities and college institutions still offer advance courses and/or programs for those who wanted to continue their studies or for those who need to re- take another subject.

The post – secondary education is not funded by the government anymore, which means that parents or the students have to pay for their tuition fees that will vary from one school to another, and depending on the course one will take.

Universities in Canada

Canadian universities are partly funded by the government to ensure high – quality standards and world - class education. Most universities in provinces and territories offer different kinds of courses or bachelor degree programs. Some universities specialize in certain courses or programs while others generally offer courses in different fields and subjects.

A Bachelor's degree takes about 3 to 5 years to complete depending on the course one will take. A Master's degree takes around 1 to 3 years, and a Doctoral degree (PhD) takes 3 years or more following a Master's degree.

Regulated professions like in the fields of law, education, accountancy, engineering, and medicine usually needs to complete a certain number of years of internship or must be able to pass a licensure exam after completing their Bachelor's degree in order to get their license or be certified.

Credential Recognition in Schools/Universities

Just like in elementary and secondary education, your credentials from your previous school whether locally or in your home country should be equivalent to the standards of a particular college institution you would enroll into. This means that for expats who wanted to continue their studies in Canada, one of the main qualifications is to have your existing credential recognized by the college/university otherwise you may have to go back another year/level.

Each college institutions and universities in different provinces and territories have their own set of admission requirements and criteria in recognizing academic credentials of foreign nationals who studied abroad. Make sure to ask help from the office of admissions so that you know the steps to take, and the requirements you'll need to take a particular course or study your chosen field. You can also hire a credential evaluator for consultation regarding these matters.

Chapter Eight: Taxes & Banking in Canada

Just like in any other countries, the Canadian government will take money from your pocket through an income tax if you're an professional employee or skilled worker, property tax (for those who have estates), and business tax (for entrepreneurs/investors). Even if you're already retired or just someone looking to stay in Canada for the short – term/temporary residency, one way or another you'll have to incur certain taxes every time you pay for goods or avail services.

As a foreigner the rules for paying taxes in Canada, and the amount will be quite different and probably even less (or more) than what you pay in your home country. This is also advantageous for people who'll be doing business in the country because they can possibly minimize their tax obligations.

It's highly recommended that you consult a tax specialist or accountant for foreign entrepreneurs wanting to start a business in Canada, so that you can choose the best option when it comes to declaring taxes for your business. This chapter will give you an overview of the taxation system in Canada. We'll also cover how the banking system works in the country, the financial services available, and other financial services you can avail.

Taxation in Canada

Canadian residents and immigrants (even those with temporary – resident visas) are obliged to pay different kinds of taxes. There are federal taxes, provincial/territorial taxes, and also municipal taxes that citizens/immigrants have to pay because it will be used to fund Canada's different programs in different sectors, ad will also be used for different services in the country.

Income Tax

Canadians and immigrants are required to pay an income tax every time they'll receive a salary. It's usually automatically deducted by the company where one works upon receipt of salary.

If you are a self – employed individual, you have the option to pay your taxes via single payment (one – time payment for the entire year) or through several payments. You should submit an Income Tax and Benefit Return to let the government know how much profit you made because this will be the basis of how much tax you'll have to pay.

For employees and self – employed individuals, filing an Income Tax and Benefit Return makes you qualified for several benefits given by the government including various provincial or territorial government programs, some of which include the following:

- Canada Child Tax Benefit (CCTB)
- Universal Child Care Benefit (UCCB)
- Goods and Services Tax (GST)
- Harmonized Sales Tax (HST)

Income tax forms are available at CRA tax services office or any post office near you. Do take note that if you are residing in Quebec, there could be differences when it comes to the federal and provincial income tax forms. Your address on the 31st of December is the place where you should file your taxes.

For temporary – resident expats considering extending their stay in the country, you need to notify the CRA because you may still need to file an income tax return for that year. The deadline for filing of taxes is every year on the 30th of April.

Business Tax

Tax returns including tax advantages and obligations for your business whether it is small or big highly depends on the type of your business or the legal structure.

For Small to Medium Businesses

If your business is registered as a sole proprietorship, partnerships including Limited Liabilities Corporation (LLC), you need to report your business profit/income in your personal income tax form (T1). Your business will represent you, and the T1 income tax return includes Form T2125 which is the Statement of Business or Professional Activities. This is what you will use to report or declare to the government your business income.

If your business is incorporated, what you need to do is file your business income tax on a T2 (Corporate Income Tax Return form). Compared to sole proprietorship and partnerships, your business is considered a separate entity from you since it's already incorporated. It'll be required to have its own income tax return. With that being said, that means you will also have to file your own T1 tax return form or your personal income tax.

For Corporations

Corporations are again considered a separate entity from their owners. It will need to have its own income tax return called the T2 (Corporate Income Tax Return form), and the owners will also need to file their own T1 personal income tax return form.

When it comes to corporate taxes, the company needs to pay federal taxes and also the provincial/territorial taxes where the company is registered.

Federal Rates:

- The basic federal rate is 38% of the taxable income
- 28% after the federal tax abatement
- 15% net tax rate (after the general tax reductions)

Provincial/ Territorial Rates:

- There are two types of income tax rates; lower rate and higher rate

- Lower rate applies to the business income that's eligible for the federal small business deduction (it includes the business limit).

- Higher rate applies to all other income

How to File an Income Tax in Canada

Unless you have an accountant, have hired a professional income tax employee or the company your working for automatically deducts your taxes, you'll need to file your own income taxes. The CRA or Canadian Revenue Agency offers different options in filing personal income taxes and business/corporate income taxes:

- For individual tax filing (T1 Personal Income Tax), you can file your tax returns by using a program called Nefile at <https://www.canada.ca/en/revenue-agency/services/e-services/e-services-businesses/gst-hst-netfile.html > as long as you meet the conditions listed on the government's website. Netfile is what Canadians use to prepare taxes for professinals/ self – employed individuals.

- For corporations, electronic filing is also available, just go directly to this website: <https://www.canada.ca/en/revenue-agency/services/e-services/e-services-businesses/corporation-internet-filing.html>

- Filing of individual tax returns can also be done manually through mail or you can personally file it at the appropriate CRA tax centers where you work/ where your business is registered.

Financial Institutions and Banking in Canada

Financial institutions and banks in Canada like *Credit Unions* and *Caisses Populaires* are safe places where you can save and grow your money. Canadian banks offer the same financial services just like in most banks around the world; they offer savings account, debit cards, credit cards, personal loans, investments, time deposits, and also function as a payment channel. There are many financial institutions in

Canada that caters both to local and foreign nationals. The banks offer a variety of financial services to individual clients as well corporations or business entities.

If your bank/ financial institution is a member of the Canadian Deposit Insurance Corporation then that means that the government will insure your savings up to CAD$100,000.

How to Open a Bank Account

You can open a bank account in Canada even if you're under the following conditions:

- If you're not currently employed
- If you don't have money to fund the account right away
- If you have poor credit history/ rating
- You have been bankrupt before

Opening an account requires you to be physically present, and you must be able to pass the needed documents, and identification that the bank will require. Below are the identification documents you need to provide, do take note the following:

- You must be able to show at least 2 pieces of ID listed in List A, or

- You must be able to show at least 1 piece of ID listed in List A, and 1 piece listed in List B, or

- You must be able to show at least 1 piece of ID listed in List A, and have someone from the bank confirm who you say you are.

IDs in List A

- A Canadian driver's licence*

- A Social Insurance Number (SIN) card

- An Old Age Security (OAS) card with your SIN

- A provincial or territorial health insurance card (except in Ontario, Prince Edward Island and Manitoba)**

- A permanent resident card or a Citizenship and Immigration Canada (CIC) form IMM 1000, IMM 1442 or IMM 5292

*Financial institutions cannot require a Quebec driver's licence for identification purposes, but you may present one if you wish.

**Financial institutions cannot require a Quebec health insurance card as a piece of identification, but you may present one if you wish.

IDs in List B

- An employee ID card with a photograph, from a known employer

- A debit card or bank card with your name and signature on it

- A Canadian credit card with your name and signature on it

- A Canadian National Institute for the Blind (CNIB) client card with your photograph and signature on it

- A valid foreign passport

Important Reminder: Unless the personal bank account you are opening pays interest, you do not need to provide your SIN to the bank. You also don't need to have a permanent address, but you need to provide proof of residency like electric bills, cable, internet or telephone bills that'll include your name and address, and must be recent.

Types of Bank Accounts

Savings and Investment Accounts

This is a type of account where you can save your money, and also have the option to switch into an investment account where your money can yield interest for a certain period of time.

Checking Accounts

Checking accounts allows a client to use checks or write checks that often includes a debit card. Usually, the transaction fees are lower, and there are no fixed monthly fees. If your employer uses a payroll deposit then you need to have a checking account so that your money can directly be deposited in your checking account.

Credit and Bank Loans

Credit cards are very useful and convenient in Canada because it is what most Canadians used in all of their transactions, and it can also be hard to purchase items if you don't have one. You should just make sure that you know how to manage your finances so that you won't have trouble paying later because interest rates can be high, and can bury you with debt.

You'll need to submit certain requirements like when you're opening a bank account but additional documents might be required. Another main requirement is a good credit history and credit score. Your credit history and credit score determines whether or not you can pay back on time. Whenever you avail a bank loan or use your credit card for purchasing, it becomes part of your credit history, and you credit score depends on how long it takes for you to pay back the money you borrowed and other factors.

Having a credit card is a great way to build credit history especially for newcomers like you. Ensure that you pay bills on time like your rent, utilities, and even your insurance premiums, tuition fees etc.

Chapter Nine: Healthcare in Canada

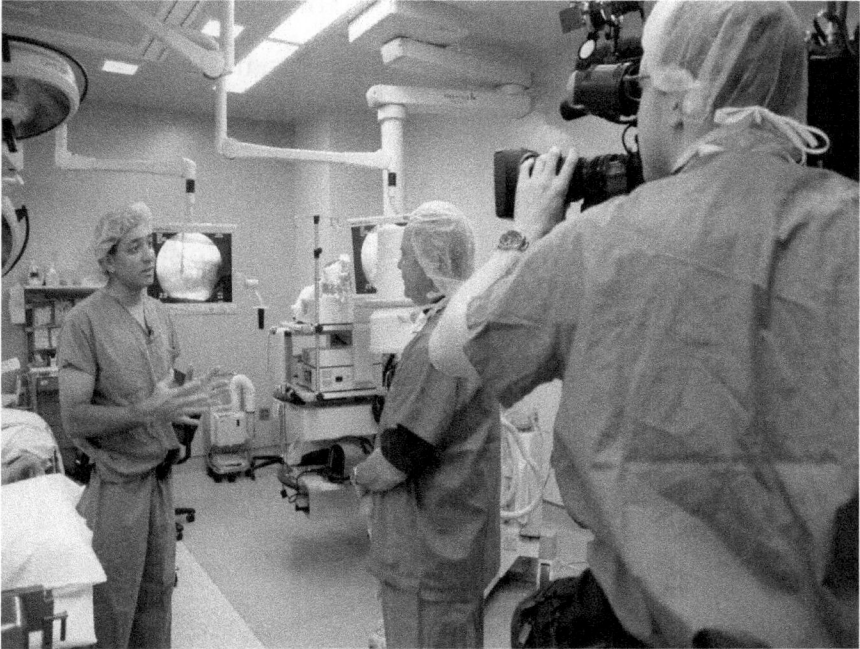

Canada's Universal Health Insurance system is what most immigrants – young and old, with families or without, and temporary or permanent residents. Canada is one of top countries in the world that provides excellent and quality health care system, it's also designed to ensure that all residents in the country whether they are citizens or immigrants have access to health care and medical facilities.

All eligible residents should apply for public health insurance to gain access to all the health care benefits as stated and approved by the government. If you are registered for Canada's public health insurance system that means that you won't need to pay in cash or directly to the hospital/clinic when you avail health – care services that are only included in the health insurance system (as there can be some restrictions).

Funds for health care are paid collectively by residents and citizens through taxes. You should show your health insurance ID or card to the health care facilities to know if you are free to avail your needed treatments or consultations.

Health Care System in Canada

One of the major differences of Canada's health care system from other countries is that instead of having only a single national healthcare plan, each province and territories have their own healthcare plan that makes up the universal health insurance system of the country. All of these plans have common standards and features but some plans/programs still vary from one place to another. Make sure that you know the medical services you can avail as well as the procedures that is in place depending on where you live because the medical coverage can vary.

There are also some restrictions or limitations when it comes to health coverage for immigrants because this will depend on your immigration status. Don't worry though because just in case there's an emergency or you need to have something checked, you can still go to hospitals/ clinics as a walked – in patient but you will most likely be charged with a fee, and you need to pay in cash.

Supplementary Health Insurance

Government health coverage in Canada provides access to most medical – related services but you may still need to avail private insurance systems for other health – related needs, this is where Supplementary Health Insurance comes in because it will pretty much cover medical needs that's not included or fully – covered in the government's plans.

Below are some examples of expenses that will need a supplementary health insurance provided by private health insurance companies or from the company you work for as part of the employee's benefits:

- Some prescription medicines
- Dental Care
- Physiotherapy (PT)
- Ambulance services
- Eyeglasses

Health Cards

In order for you to access the health care coverage of the government, you need to be registered, and have a health insurance ID/card. This will be given in the province/ territory where you are residing. Health card is very important because without these you won't be able to access healthcare benefits for free, you will of course receive medical attention but you must pay the hospital/clinic in cash.

Acquiring health cards in Canada will vary depending on the requirements you will need to pass, and your immigration status.

Medical and Dental Services in Canada

Finding Doctors

Many Canadians have their own family physicians for their medical needs and consultations. Family doctors provides general health care for patients including check – ups, preventative health care, laboratory tests, and other general medical needs that won't need major or specialize treatments. Your family physician will refer you to a specialize doctor if need be.

You need to just make a call or drop by the office if you want to make an appointment. There are also certain conditions that will apply once a family doctor accepts you so make sure to inquire about that. If you want to see a physician without an appointment, you can go to your community health center to see if one is available.

Finding Dentists

Finding a dentist in Canada is much easier than finding family physicians. Accepting new patients is not a problem. However, dental care is not covered by the government so it's best that you get a supplementary insurance for coverage or just pay in cash.

Vaccinations or Immunizations

Vaccines are needed especially for kids because it serves as protection from getting serious illnesses brought about by virus, bacteria or other diseases. Each province and territory in Canada has its own immunization programs that are being offered by both children and adults, and covers a number of illnesses. Make sure to ask your family doctor about the vaccines you or your children need to take as it will depend on one's age and condition.

For immigrants, Canada will need vaccination certificates or proof that you have been vaccinated for particular diseases if you're coming from certain countries like in Africa. For more information about this go to <www.phac-aspc.gc.ca/im/index-eng.php>

Emergency and Ambulance Services

In cases of emergencies, you can go to the emergency room of your nearest hospital or call 911 if you need assistance or immediate medical attention. Emergency services are free in hospitals (as long as you are covered by the health care system); otherwise you'll need to pay for it.

The ambulance services are not covered by the government so you either pay for it in cash unless your private insurance covers it. The price varies in each provinces and territories.

Medical Surveillance for Newly Arrived Immigrants

During the immigration medical exams required to for expats, you may have been told to report to the public health authorities when you arrive in the country, this procedure is known as medical surveillance. You should do this within 1 month or 30 days of your arrival. This is to check if you are in good health condition and you're not carrying deadly diseases/viruses from other countries. You may be advised to seek medical treatment or do consultations if need be. Once completing the medical assessment, no changes in your health will affect your immigration status.

Pregnancy and Maternity Benefits

Contact and visit your local health service centers so that they can recommend a doctor or nurse to help you during your pregnancy. Health service centers can also provide you with information about the following:

- Sexual Health

- Pregnancy/ Childbirth

- Prenatal Development

- Maternity

- Birth Certificates Registration

- Prenatal Courses

- Nursing Care

Working moms can take a maternity leave from their employer for a set period of time. Employment Insurance provides benefits for eligible soon to be moms and dads.

Healthcare for Expat Retiree and Seniors

Each provinces and territories in Canada have special coverage for seniors and for those eligible foreign nationals who are already seniors. Restrictions will apply in different places regarding on how long you must become a resident in a particular province/territory to avail or maintain the covered health benefits.

- You must be physically present in the province/territory for a number of days in a 12 – month or 1 year period.
- Your permanent address and principal home should be in that particular province/territory.

Meeting these terms is necessary because it will provide you with medical coverage, health services done at home, and even when you are travelling in other provinces or outside the country. Medical benefits that are covered for seniors usually include the following:

Eye Care

- 1 eye exam by an optometrist per year. Some provinces also offer 1 color vision testing every year.
- Cataract surgery

Not Included:

- Eyeglasses
- Contact Lenses

Hearing

- Hearing tests
- Hearing aids (partial cost only)

Not Included:

- Evaluation of hearing aids
- Audiologist services

Physiotherapy

- Therapy (either in the hospital or license PT clinic).

Not Included:

- Some services provided in private hospitals/clinics.

Dental Care Services

- Some dental surgery that needed to be performed in the hospital

Not Included:

- Dental services in the dentist's office

Medical Equipment

- Medical supplies such as the following:
  - mobility aids
  - insulin dependent supplies
  - respiratory equipment
  - oxygen/ oxygen delivery equipment
  - wheelchairs
  - orthopedic braces
  - breathing aids

Not Included:

- Equipment and supplies that are not listed above (varies from one province to another)

Chronic Care Services

- Includes the hospital room, and other basic necessities aside from the medical care being given. The rate is determined by the monthly income and also the number of dependents of the patient.

Home Care Services

- Covers the following services (partial coverage only):
    - Nursing Care
    - Physiotherapy
    - Personal Support Services (bathing, dressing, meal preparation)
    - Palliative Care

Chapter Ten: Preparing for Your Relocation in Canada

You and your family will need to do careful planning before, and after you moved out of your home country, and moved into your new home in Canada. Your relocation plan will highly depend on your own living situations but key factors such as your status whether you're single or married, age, purpose, and financial capacity will definitely influence the complexity of your relocation.

Those who are young, single, and working individuals will have a less complicated situation when it comes to moving into another country compared to those who will move with their families and those expat retirees who may need someone to look after them.

Every immigrant's situation is different, keep in mind that the list and tips provided here is only an indication of the things you need to do at different stages. Some of the items may not be relevant to your situation but preparation is key in making a successful transition. If you're a refugee, the Canadian government will be the one to instruct you what to do once you arrive in the country; the government is also in charge of supporting you and your needs during the immigration process.

This chapter will focus on all the most important things you need to consider before you arrive in Canada. This is a practical checklist for you and your family so that you'll know what to do, and will have enough time to take care of your unique situations, and so that you won't miss out anything. There are many aspects when relocating to a foreign country; this pre – moving checklist will guide you at the different planning stage of your relocation including how to legally move to Canada with your family as well as your possessions. This chapter will also cover what you need to do once you arrive (your first 2 weeks), and once you're already settled in (your first 2 months) as there'll be immigration requirements you still need to accomplish.

Tips Before Your Immigrate to Canada

Tip #1: Gather all the official documents and immigration requirements for you or your family coming with you. Make sure that before you leave your home country, you have already obtained original copies of the general documents listed because it's much harder to obtain it after you left your country of origin.

General Documents:
- o Birth Certificate/s (for you/your spouse/children/relatives)

- o Passport
- o Identification Cards
- o Marriage/Divorced/Death Certificate/s (of diseased spouse)
- o Diplomas
- o Transcript records
- o Certificates (education or employment)
- o Adoption Records (for adopted children)
- o Vaccination Records/Certificates
- o Medical Records (including laboratory results, other necessary test results, prescriptions, dental records etc.)
- o Driver's License / International Driving Permit

- Not all of these documents are needed right away but it is better if you prepare all of them for future reference.
- You should also make sure that your documents/ certifications are translated either in English or French if it's written in other languages other than Canada's official languages.

- If you're going to reside in Quebec, it's better to translate the documents in French. Just choose a translation agency with a good reputation in your home country.
- If your family is going to come at a later date, it's also best that you bring original copies of their documents.

Tip #2: Learn the language and improve your communication skills.

Most immigrants especially those from non – English speaking countries are required to take certain language test/s before arriving in Canada particularly those who are immigrant workers. Make sure that your English or French speaking skills is understandable because it'll be one of the most important tools you need to have if you wanted to successfully settle in the country and easily find a job. If you're going to reside in Quebec and other French speaking communities, you'll need to at least know basic French.

Tip #3: Plan where you will stay once you arrive in Canada or during your first few days.

If your house or the place you're going to rent is not yet ready once you arrive, then make sure that you have an alternative place to stay in such as a hotel or other transient houses you/ your family can stay in temporarily that is near your neighborhood.

Tip #4: Prepare your documents for employment.

This is particularly for people who are immigrant workers. Before you arrive in Canada, make sure that you acquire your educational and professional certificates to ensure that your qualifications are recognized in Canada. Ensure to prepare the following general documents during the immigration process/ employment process:

- o Diplomas
- o Professional Certificates
- o Letter of References from your previous employers
- o Other necessary documents needed by the company

Tip #5: Learn Canada's education system.

If you're an immigrant looking to study in Canada or continue your study in higher education, make sure that you learn about Canada's education system. Parents should also take note of the deadlines for applying, registering, paying for tuition fees, and the schooling schedules especially if they have young children. Students should also prepare for the documents needed as required by the school/university.

Tip #6: Purchase a private health insurance for you and your family while waiting for your health card.

Even if the government will provide coverage for immigrants who are permanent residents already, it's still highly recommended that you purchase a health insurance from private providers because it might take some time (around 3 to 6 months) before you receive your health insurance cards/ grants from the government. This will protect you and your family just in case you get sick or an emergency happens in your first few months in the country.

Tip #7: Do research and learn everything you can about the place where you're going to relocate.

Aside from reviewing this book, it's best that you do your own research regarding the province/ territory you're going to reside in so that you'll know what to expect once you arrive. It's also best that you know the climate/seasons in your chosen area so that you can already prepare the clothes, and maybe plan activities ahead of time.

Tip #8: Learn about the customs, laws, and culture as well as your civil rights and responsibilities as a Canadian resident.

As a resident of Canada, you should make sure that you know the rules and regulations in the country as well as your civil rights and responsibilities so that you'll become a law – abiding immigrant/citizen, and also contribute to the betterment of Canada's society.

Things to Do in Your First Few Weeks (1 – 2 weeks)

- Know where to get the different sources of information that could help you settle in your chosen area. This will include different places/landmarks in Canada, community centers, nearest hospitals, schools, transportation areas, utilities, and knowledge about other basic necessities.

- Make sure to visit the nearest immigrant – serving organization because this is the office which will cater for all immigrant needs you may have.

- Apply for a health insurance card once you arrive so that it can be processed as soon as possible. You'll need this to access your health care benefits.

- Apply for a Social Insurance Number (SIN) especially if you're planning to find a job in the country.

- Make sure to get your permanent resident card from the Citizenship and Immigration Canada (CIC) office. Just provide them with your Canadian address.

- Open a Canadian bank account

- Familiarize yourself around your neighborhood, town, city or province. Get to know the best routes, nearest services, and access points especially the transportation areas so that you can easily navigate and go from one place to another.

- Learn how you can access the communication lines such as telephones, internet, and Canada's mailing system.

- Know all the important numbers in your area like the emergency services, ambulance services, and the police department in case you'll need assistance.

- Get to know the people living in your neighborhood. Introduce yourself to them if you have the time, and make friends so that they can help you adjust to your new life.

Things to Do in Your First Few Months (1 – 3 months)

- Now is a good time to already find a job because you already have an idea of the Canadian way of living. You can begin your job search by looking at job postings online or in community centers. Ensure to prepare your resume or CV, cover letter, previous employment references and other qualifying documents.

- You can also take free language classes (c/o taxpayers/government) to improve your English or French speaking skills. Inquire in your immigrant – serving organizations about this.

- If you lack qualifications or credentials for your work or your studies, then it's best that you learn about various education options in educational institutions so that you can continue your studies or acquire certifications.

- Obtain a Canadian Driver's License if you want to drive in Canada. You'll need to prepare your immigrant documents, and you should also pass the written and practical tests for you to acquire a license.

- Find a family physician and dentist in your area for your medical/dental needs. Locate your nearest hospital/clinic as well so that you know where to go during emergency situations.

Basic Travel Essentials

This chapter will provide you with a quick rundown of the other basic essential things you need to know. We hope this book helped you in preparing for your relocation to Canada, and provided you with the knowledge you need on how to become an immigrant in the Maple Country! Most importantly, we hoped that this book has encouraged you to try out a different culture, and consider settling with the warm and welcoming Canadians!

Canada Basic Essentials

Here's a quick run – down of the basic essentials when travelling to Canada:

- **Capital City:** Ottawa, Ontario
- **Population:** 35 Million (as of 2016)
- **Government:** Parliamentary democracy; Constitutional Monarchy
- **Current Leader:** Prime Minister Justin Trudeau (2015 to present day).
- **Religion:** 67% Roman Catholics; 23% no religion
- **Currency:** Canadian Dollar ($)
- **Language:** English; French
- **Electricity:** 110 to 120 Volts (60 hertz), and the outlets require 3 – pronged North American Ground plugs.
- **ATMs/Money:** Visa, Master Card, American Express are widely accepted; traveller's cheques and foreign currencies are also accepted in major shops/restaurants

- **General Entry Requirements:**
  - Valid Passport
  - Tourist Visa/ Residence Visas/Permits
  - Return Tickets
  - Hotel bookings/reservations
  - Letter of invitation (if applicable)
  - Other travel documents (bank statements; proof of sufficient funds etc.)

- **Climate:** Usually very cold all year round, and experiences long winters, heavy snow storms, and cool summers.
- **Tipping:** at least 10 – 15% tip for local waiters/bars/restaurants if service charge is not yet included. At least 15 – 20% if you are dining in international establishments.
- **Communication:**
  - **To make calls in Canada and the USA:**
    If you want to make a call across the country, simply dial the 10 digit number (area code + number). In certain regions, you only dial the

last seven digits of the number (without the area code). To make a long-distance call to a number in Canada, dial 1 + area code + number.

o **To make calls international calls:**
Just dial 011 (this is the "exit code") + the country code + the area code + the number.

- **Public Holidays**
    - Jan 1: New Year's Day
    - Feb 19: Family Day
    - Feb 5: Day of Constitution
    - Mar 23: Victoria Day
    - July 1: Canada Day
    - August 1: August Civic Holiday
    - September 5: Labor Day
    - October 10: Thanksgiving Day
    - December 25: Christmas Day

PHOTO REFERENCES

Foreword Page Photo by user toptop54 via Pixabay.com, https://pixabay.com/en/canada-national-park-flag-maple-55981/

Page 1 Photo by user ShawShank61 via Pixabay.com, https://pixabay.com/en/empress-hotel-victoria-inner-harbor-1271462/

Page 7 Photo by user Graham – H via Pixabay.com, https://pixabay.com/en/water-nature-seashore-sea-summer-3066330/

Page 9 Photo by user werner22brigitte via Pixabay.com, https://pixabay.com/en/science-world-false-creek-vancouver-210775/

Page 12 Photo by user spencer via Pixabay.com, https://pixabay.com/en/soldiers-musket-canada-war-civil-144553/

Page 16 Photo by user AlainAudet via Pixabay.com, https://pixabay.com/en/winter-landscape-sunset-twilight-2995987/

Page 19 Photo by user StockSnap via Pixabay.com, https://pixabay.com/en/girls-women-people-canadian-flags-2557255/

Page 26 Photo by user Number 10 via Flickr.com, https://www.flickr.com/photos/number10gov/36507688673/

Page 30 Photo by user 12019 via Pixabay.com, https://pixabay.com/en/toronto-canada-city-urban-skyline-2183706/

Page 38 Photo by user Etereuti via Pixabay.com, https://pixabay.com/en/canada-north-america-national-flag-1157521/

Page 56 Photo by user Benson Kua via Flickr.com, https://www.flickr.com/photos/bensonkua/15260982071/

Page 62 Photo by user werner22brigitte via Pixabay.com, https://pixabay.com/en/vancouver-city-skyscraper-houseboat-56648/

Page 67 Photo by user 12019 via Pixabay.com, https://pixabay.com/en/lake-ontario-canada-hdr-fall-1581897/

Page 72 Photo by user Aurusdorus via Pixabay.com, https://pixabay.com/en/frontenac-qu%C3%A9bec-castle-canada-2257154/

Page 81 Photo by user jameswheeler via Pixabay.com, https://pixabay.com/en/bc-beautiful-bridge-2297205/

Page 87 Photo by user ErikaWittlieb via Pixabay.com, https://pixabay.com/en/canada-government-legislature-2687490/

Page 95 Photo by user Jung R via Pixabay.com, https://pixabay.com/en/moraine-lake-banff-canada-alberta-2314026/

Page 101 Photo by user Pedro Szekely via Flickr.com,
https://www.flickr.com/photos/pedrosz/29659162631/

Page 104 Photo by user richoz via Pixabay.com,
https://pixabay.com/en/saint-donat-canada-lake-quebec-488217/

Page 121 Photo by user Dezalb via Pixabay.com,
https://pixabay.com/en/canada-quebec-old-town-shops-store-2200776/

Page 126 Photo by user Patrice_Audet via Pixabay.com,
https://pixabay.com/en/qu%C3%A9bec-city-quebec-monument-canada-552069/

Page 130 Photo by user Funky Focus via Pixabay.com,
https://pixabay.com/en/mobile-phone-smartphone-3d-1875813/

Page 145 Photo by user Tumisu via Pixabay.com,
https://pixabay.com/en/contact-us-contact-email-phone-2993000/

Page 159 Photo by user Public Domain Pictures via Pixabay.com,

https://pixabay.com/en/downtown-toronto-buildings-canada-16916/

Page 167 Photo by user Free – Photos via Pixabay.com,

https://pixabay.com/en/urban-people-crowd-citizens-438393/

Page 177 Photo by user Garry Knight via Flickr.com,

https://www.flickr.com/photos/garryknight/3699199592/

Page 185 Photo by user Jeff S. Photography via Flickr.com,

https://www.flickr.com/photos/jeff_sch/6836636554/

Page 193 Photo by user Anita Hart via Flickr.com,

https://www.flickr.com/photos/anitakhart/2737188217/

Page 202 Photo by user Brent Eades via Flickr.com,

https://www.flickr.com/photos/59355637@N00/7343280476/

Page 211 Photo by user Vancouver Coastal Health via Flickr.com,

https://www.flickr.com/photos/vancouvercoastalhealth/5712210706/

Page 217 Photo by user Monika Designs via Pixabay.com, https://pixabay.com/en/cottage-lake-water-nature-summer-1550083/

Page 230 Photo by user Keith JJ via Flickr.com, https://pixabay.com/en/canada-day-canada-flag-celebration-1485418/

REFERENCES

About Ontario – CanadaVisa.com

https://www.canadavisa.com/about-ontario.html

Accommodation in Canada – Expat Arrivals

http://www.expatarrivals.com/canada/accommodation-in-canada

A guide to doing business in Canada – Cadogantate.com

https://www.cadogantate.com/en/moving-services/news/guide-to-doing-business-canada

Buying Property in Canada – Expat Arrivals

http://www.expatarrivals.com/canada/buying-property-in-canada

Canada's Four Seasons – TripSavvy.com

https://www.tripsavvy.com/four-seasons-in-canada-1482200

Canada - Self-Employment and Business Start Ups – ExpatFocus.com

http://www.expatfocus.com/expatriate-canada-self-employment

Corporation Tax Rates – Canada.ca

https://www.canada.ca/en/revenue-agency/services/tax/businesses/topics/corporations/corporation-tax-rates.html

Communications for Expat in Canada – ExpatBriefing.com

https://www.expatbriefing.com/country/canada/living/communications-for-expats-in-canada.html

Cost of living in Toronto, Canada – Expatistan.com

https://www.expatistan.com/cost-of-living/toronto

How to choose a cell phone plan in Canada – Moving2Canada.com

https://moving2canada.com/cell-phone-plan-in-canada/

How to Find a Job in Canada as a Foreigner – VisaHunter.com

http://www.visahunter.com/articles/how-to-find-a-job-in-canada-as-a-foreigner

Life after retirement: Health care costs require careful planning – Financial Post

http://business.financialpost.com/personal-finance/retirement/your-life-after-retirement-health-care-costs-require-careful-planning

The best, cheapest Canadian cellphone plan out there: 2013 edition – Global News

https://globalnews.ca/news/676741/whats-the-best-cheapest-canadian-cellphone-plan-out-there/

Welcome to Canada: What You Should Know – Citizenship and Immigration Canada

https://www.canada.ca/content/dam/ircc/migration/ircc/english/pdf/pub/welcome.pdf

Work Permits for Canada – Expat Arrivals

http://www.expatarrivals.com/canada/work-permits-for-canada

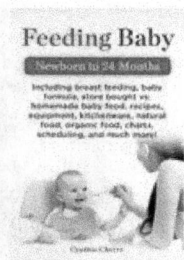

Feeding Baby
Cynthia Cherry
978-1941070000

Axolotl
Lolly Brown
978-0989658430

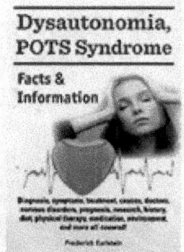

Dysautonomia, POTS
Syndrome
Frederick Earlstein
978-0989658485

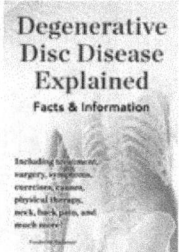

Degenerative Disc
Disease Explained
Frederick Earlstein
978-0989658485

Sinusitis, Hay Fever,
Allergic Rhinitis Explained
Frederick Earlstein
978-1941070024

Wicca
Riley Star
978-1941070130

Zombie Apocalypse
Rex Cutty
978-1941070154

Capybara
Lolly Brown
978-1941070062

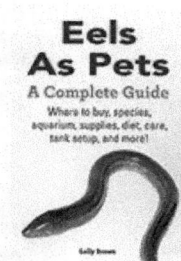

Eels As Pets
Lolly Brown
978-1941070167

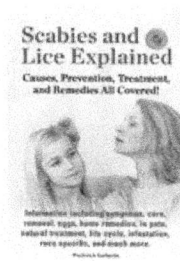

Scabies and Lice Explained
Frederick Earlstein
978-1941070017

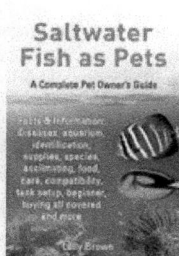

Saltwater Fish As Pets
Lolly Brown
978-0989658461

Torticollis Explained
Frederick Earlstein
978-1941070055

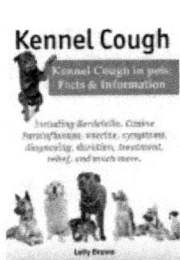

Kennel Cough
Lolly Brown
978-0989658409

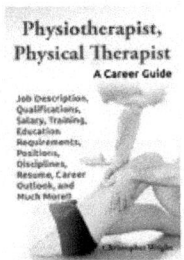

Physiotherapist, Physical
Therapist
Christopher Wright
978-0989658492

Rats, Mice, and Dormice
As Pets
Lolly Brown
978-1941070079

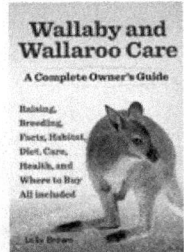

Wallaby and Wallaroo Care
Lolly Brown
978-1941070031

Bodybuilding Supplements
Explained
Jon Shelton
978-1941070239

Demonology
Riley Star
978-19401070314

Pigeon Racing
Lolly Brown
978-1941070307

Dwarf Hamster
Lolly Brown
978-1941070390

Cryptozoology
Rex Cutty
978-1941070406

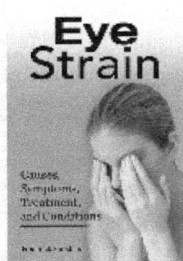

Eye Strain
Frederick Earlstein
978-1941070369

Inez The Miniature Elephant
Asher Ray
978-1941070353

Vampire Apocalypse
Rex Cutty
978-1941070321

www.ingramcontent.com/pod-product-compliance
Lightning Source LLC
Chambersburg PA
CBHW071415090426
42737CB00011B/1465